GANGER, GUARD AND SIGNALMAN

GANGER GUARD AND SIGNALMAN

Working memories of the Settle & Carlisle

Dick Fawcett

BRADFORD BARTON

ISBN 0 85153 397 3

set and printed by CTP Ltd for Top Link Ltd
for the publishers
D. BRADFORD BARTON LTD
Trethellan House · Truro · England

BD9433

THE AUTHOR started work for the L.M.S.R. in 1932, initially as a mason working on one of the viaducts near the high summit of the Settle & Carlisle. This was followed by a period as a ganger, also based on Garsdale – otherwise Hawes Junction. From this, he progressed to the ranks of the local goods guards, ranging not only over the S. & C. itself between Carlisle and Hellifield, but also over the L. & Y. route from the latter as far as Salford and beyond, and out to Carnforth and Barrow. A transfer as porter/signalman at Bolton Abbey for a spell was followed by promotion to signalman at a number of boxes in the area from Skipton to Ribblehead and on the 'Old Road' from Settle Junction through to Clapham and Lancaster. On relief work, he saw duty at almost every box within these limits and this highly personal account of his two decades 'on and off the locker' are recorded here in his own homespun style. In all, before retirement, he saw more than thirty years service on and around the Settle & Carlisle, from steam right through to the days of the diesels. In that time he became a well-known local character – not only as a railwayman but also as a poacher of some quite considerable repute. He now lives at Green Close near Clapham alongside the track-bed of the former Ingleton branch, in a house he built himself on the site of former railway cottages. In these pages, alas, space does not permit inclusion of any of the tales of his poaching days and ways, or of the wildlife of the Dales he loves so well . . .

CONTENTS

CHAPTER ONE

My Early Days as a Ganger

I STARTED WORK for the L.M.S. Railway in 1932 as a Grade II mason, working on the Moorcock Viaduct – or Dandra Mire Viaduct, as some chose to call it. I was stationed at nearby Garsdale, or as I had previously known it, Hawes Junction; and in the remainder of these pages I intend always to refer to it as Hawes Junction.

We were a gang of eight men and a foreman – Walter Fellows, a bricklayer from Leeds. Our job was to repair the pillars and coping stones, plus the replacement of any rotten brickwork under the arches. We worked suspended high up in cages raised by hand-winches and secured by iron 'cat heads', which were fastened under the running lines and extended up over the coping stones.

That summer was very wet and cold and we had some pretty miserable times, with the wind and rain blowing through those arches at the top of Garsdale Valley and from the other direction up Wensleydale. I was dreading winter on that job, and it was approaching fast. I had experienced some of the winters in that area previously. Moreover, there was some likelihood of members of our gang being laid off for winter, so I made application to be transferred into the Slip & Drainage Gang based at Garsdale, and I was accepted.

Eight men and a ganger; 'Slip & Drainage' was our official title, also 'Gang 203', I believe. We were also known as the 'Rough Gang' or 'Gamsby's Gang'. Joe Gamsby, our ganger, was a great fellow and could tackle any job. He had been a sergeant in the First World War in a Gurkha Regiment and many were the stories he told of those brave little fighting men. He was often heard to say he would willingly swap the eight of us for four of his little Gurkhas . . .

We put in and repaired drains through Helm Tunnel, Ormside; through Griseburn Ballast Sidings; Crosby Garrett; Birkett Tunnel, between Mallerstang and Kirkby Stephen; Fred Cutting near Appersett on the Hawes branch line; Shotlock Slip; Lund's Slip; and many other places. 'Slip' was the shortened version of the word 'landslide' up there.

Those first few months in Gamsby's Gang almost made me into a nervous wreck. We were digging out and putting in a new drain on the down line side of Birkett Tunnel. There is a swamp on the moor above the tunnel and there was a lot of seepage water getting onto the lines.

The top of the rail is never as good inside a tunnel as it is outside, owing to the darkness, which creates bad viewing for the lengthmen, and consequently trains tend to rock badly. We would be working on the drain between the sleeper-ends and the tunnel wall (a width of about two feet between these two) when the Look-out Man would blow his horn and shout "Train on the down line." We would make a rapid scramble for the manholes built into the walls for protection. Then the train would be upon us at a great speed on the falling gradient, with the whistle blowing to warn us.

The speed of the train and the slight bad repairing often shook huge cobs of coal off the tender and these would bounce alongside and break up into pieces, peppering us as we crouched in our recesses with our backs to the line. I was terrified.

A lot of engines were coaled before leaving Leeds for Glasgow and lumps of coal could balance on the edges of the tenders all the way from there, but they would be almost certain to fall off when passing through Birkett.

Trains on the up line were going much slower but we had to take cover just the same in case one suddenly appeared on the down line. After the passage of an up train we also had to keep in our manholes until the smoke had cleared. A down train, however, could soon clear the tunnel of smoke.

The week I started in the gang I took possession of No. 2 Moorcock Cottages, owned by the L.M.S. Railway for the use of their employees. I had always been a light sleeper and it was a new experience, living right next to the main line. I would just drop off to sleep – perhaps having a nightmare about the trains of the day – when the trains of the night were coming at me from both directions. The up trains were the worst, because they came so suddenly out of the deep cutting at the south end of Moor Cock Tunnel . . . but I got used to it after a while.

We had occasion to work in and walk through Rise Hill and Blea Moor tunnels from both directions many times. And I can tell you it was a weird experience – the Chamber of Horrors would be soothing after a day in either of those. Everything dead, solid and black; the air full of sulphur, even when the tunnel was clear of trains or smoke. A lot of men had, at different times, taken refuge in a man-hole and, after a train had passed, started walking back in mistake, the way they had come. There was, however, a way of telling the direction – the wooden keys were knocked into the chairs from the side from which the train would approach, but nobody had to walk anywhere on the railway with their backs to the traffic, whatever job they were doing. If the keys had been put in from the other side, the vibration of the passing train would have shaken them out.

We would be working quietly away when one of the regular tunnel gang would say, "A train just entering the north end of the tunnel." Then a few minutes later he might say, "Look out lads, there is one coming in from the other end."

I used to think it queer how they knew, for they were never wrong. We had to be doubly sure, for sometimes when a train was passing on the line at our side, another could be passing on the opposite line and we couldn't hear it. And, take my word for it, there can be no noisier experience than being in the centre of a railway tunnel when a train is passing through.

I soon learned to sense when one was entering the tunnel, by the slight pressure on my ear drums which increased as the train approached. If another came in from the other end, I could feel the pressure increasing from both sides. Each train was preceded also by a faint faraway rumble long before reaching us in the tunnel.

If the latter was full of smoke it would be pushed along in front of a train which would also be laying its own smoke screen. This would follow along until a train in the opposite direction would start pushing it back again. In those days on the Settle & Carlisle line we had a train more or less every twenty minutes, so the air never got cleared of smoke and fumes. For these minor inconveniences, the regular tunnel gang had the sum of two-shillings-and-sixpence above the outside men, and also a soap ration. Their title in those days was platelayer, a name I shall use when the occasions arise, although I believe they come under the title of lengthmen now.

I could watch from the Ingleton-Ribblehead road and see the smoke ventilators on top of Blea Moor Tunnel and I could have told if there were one or two trains in the tunnel below, where they were, and when they passed each other. This was determinable by the smoke idling or being pushed out rapidly with two coming towards each other swiftly; or by drawing some of the smoke back inside after they had passed the smoke shafts.

And did we come out of those holes black, just our teeth and the whites of our eyes showing!

But it wasn't all work in those places – most weekends we worked with Appleby Relaying Gang, as sometimes through the week they got behind with a job.

About one day a week we would be with Carlisle ballast train, putting down materials for ourselves or other gangs, and moving theirs or our tackle to other locations. This was a new experience for me and I loved the ballast train days. Actually, that train was booked to the P. Way Dept. every day except Saturday all the year round.

Some days we did very little work – ten minutes maybe – then into the siding for a goods or an express to pass or perhaps several trains would have to pass before a signalman would let us out again for a short while. What flaps some signalmen could get into if they were being pestered by the ballast train for a few days!

The winters seemed long and the days short there at Hawes Junction, Dent and Aisgill – the places where we regularly worked. We did seem to get more snow, rain, winds and mist than I have experienced since! We spent many snug days in the cabins during this kind of weather and in winter did not turn out to work until it was light enough to see comfortably, about 8.30, whilst in the darker days of winter we were back in the cabins by about 3.30pm. Quite a few of the Platelayers' Gangers were getting near to retirement. They had a lot of railway service, had seen a lot, heard a lot, and were keen to tell of their experiences. Jim Metcalfe used to tell of his experiences and the scenes he saw in those two awful train crashes . . . one near Quarry Cottages, Lunds, on Christmas Eve 1910 (less than two miles from his home at Aisgill) on the down-line, and the second crash on the up-line about 100 yards north of Aisgill signal-box up distant signal.

He was called out of bed to assist at the crash at Lunds and told how Signalman Sutton, on night turn duty at Hawes Junction box, had two light engines on hand after each had piloted up expresses from Carlisle. To save one extra block section, the engines were coupled and sent to the down line starting signal to await acceptance from Aisgill. Then he apparently forgot about them.

Some time after, when getting the Train Entering Section signal for the down express from the signalman at Dent he offered it to Aisgill. It was accepted and he pulled all his signals off on the down line.

The two coupled engines moved off when seeing the signal drop, but in less than two miles the fast-moving express caught up with them and disaster struck.

Jim and his mates from the other cottages at Aisgill rushed along the line, aware that something terrible had happened by the glow in the sky and, though they did all they could, they were fighting a losing battle.

The second train crash, north of Aisgill, was heard by Jim when in bed. He rushed to the bedroom window, and could see flames beginning to show over the railway bridge and could clearly hear the screaming. The remainder he would not talk about. I believe the last carriage of the train that was stopped was standing right under the bridge when the engine of the second train ran into it: the underside and walls of the bridge still show the effect of that fire by the blistered and cracked stonework.

He was with some of the earliest rescuers, and their hands were blistered and clothes almost burnt off as they tried to save as many people as possible before the fire reached them in the shattered wooden carriages. He had some souvenirs that did not warrant handing in. He shaved with a razor all his life after, which he told me had belonged to a baron who was shaving himself when he was killed in the crash whilst returning to London after grouse shooting in Scotland.

Years after, platelayers used to find small articles, including sovereigns and half-sovereigns when they were repairing the lines and weeding at the site of the crash. Each spring, when the railway banks were burnt the men made a practice of looking the ground over and they still found the occasional coin around the pieces of ground where the dead had lain.

Jim once also showed me a heap – several barrow-loads – of metal-clinkers tipped near the wall next to the road; these had been brass carriage door handles mixed with copper parts burned up together with the under ballast, which had later been gathered up and dumped.

It would be hard to find such men as these gangers today. No beating about the bush; when we were told to do a job, we got on with it. They called a spade a spade, and some of the things they called us younger men were not as complimentary as being called a 'spade'.

They, and most of the platelayers, were old Midland railwaymen and many and often were the words used complaining about the new system (the L.M.S.). "Should never have come" . . . "Now the good old days have gone" . . . "The Railway is finished" . . . and "Look at the men we have to put up with now." Our headquarters were still Hawes Junction to them, and always would be. I try to be fair to them by calling it Hawes Junction.

The platelayers' cabins were warm homely places, placed perhaps half a mile from each other over the various lengths. One gang's area was called a 'length'. At the station there were four, where the three lengths met – Ted's Cabin, Tom's Cabin, Adam's Cabin, and one for us when we were working at home or on Saturday mornings when the half-day working didn't warrant travelling away. Ours was called the Gangster's Cabin.

Fires were lit a few days before the lads would be working from any particular cabin, to dispel dampness. There was always plenty of coal, supplied by the Permanent Way Department. If for some reason we were getting short, any of the engine-drivers would throw us a heap off if they were standing in the station or siding. Away from the station there was generally plenty lying around which had fallen from the tenders, whilst some of the inexperienced firemen could scatter it about a bit off the footplate until they got competent. Then again, some of the drivers were so proud of a clean footplate that they would not allow their firemen to hammer a large cob of coal into small pieces. "Just throw it off the side. Push it off at the next cabin," they would say. "But make sure there is nobody working on the side of the line."

There were a lot of days in winter when we were confined to our cabin owing to mists or rain. Our chaps were usually busy 'carding' on these occasions; failing that they would be lying around sleeping, so I would wander into one of the other cabins for a change of company.

One particular day I was in Ted Wilson's cabin, which was a few yards below the turntable. He told me about a light engine that had turned ready to run back to Carlisle. It had come down the short road between the turntable road and the main line, and then stood waiting at the dummy or ground signal to be let out onto the main line when the signalman decided. The latter pulled the down main line signals off for a through train. The driver of the light engine, forgetting for a minute where he was, saw the starting signal in front of him come off, and put his engine into motion. It moved forward into the stop blocks and toppled down the bank, arriving at the bottom on its side with the smokebox still pointing towards Carlisle.

The following Sunday a steam crane had come from Carlisle to salvage the engine but only managed to get it the right side up. The next weekend after that the Carlisle crane came again and was assisted by another large one from Derby Works, but they were still beaten with it – the engine was settling more into the mire. The third Sunday they were still unable to get the engine lifted. Anyone who has read about the building of Dandra Mire Viaduct will understand, because the engine was bogged down in the same stuff. On this particular Sunday, the bank was showing signs of slipping with the two heavy cranes on the top, tugging away at the dead-weight at the bottom. The casualty was an old Durran Hill (Carlisle) engine and the old girl kept sinking deeper, so it was finally decided the Loco Department would waste no more time upon it. So, it was left there – and still is . . .

Whilst Ted Wilson was telling me this, I must have seemed unbelieving because his second man – Billy Winn – spoke up seriously and said, "It's right, what he is telling you." To prove it, Ted took me to see for myself. After rooting about for a while amongst some small willows and pulling the long grass away we uncovered the top of a locomotive chimney. To put all doubt out of my mind. I went back to it a few days after, dug down a bit more, uncovered the smokebox top and cleaned the inside of the chimney out as far as I could reach.

I seem to remember he said it went down the bank in the early 1900s, but I have nobody to ask now. Lots of spent ballast had been thrown down the bank between the engine going down and the year Ted took me to see it. Lots more could have been thrown down since.

I cannot remember if it was Ted Wilson or Adam Rudd that was in the signal-box flagging or protecting the obstructed section between Hawes Junction and Aisgill after signalman Sutton made his terrible mistake. He said it was awful to see the poor man – and I have often thought since that it must have been terrible for the signalman taking over from him. Relief would be provided at the earliest moment.

The apparatus for signalling at that time was the old Midland Railway Free Block, and with that type a careless signalman could easily have a train smash on his hands.

After this second accident, the Midland Railway installed the infallible Rotary Block: One Line Clear, one Pull off; Track circuits at the home and starting signals; Rule 55. If these had been in operation at the time, neither of these accidents would have occurred.

I do not know if Rule 55 was in operation at that time; if it had been the fireman of the second engine ought to have gone back to the signalbox, reminded the signalman that he had two engines standing at the starting signal for Aisgill and then signed his name in the Train Register Book.

Fog or snow was a different business from rain for us gangers. If it was foggy, some of the men had to drop what they were doing and report to the signalman for Fog Emergency Regulations, then immediately take up their positions at the signals they were allocated. Other men went home to get their rest, before they were required for similar duties should the fog persist.

With heavy snow it was more serious, for Fog Signalling Regulations came into operation. It was as hard for an engine-driver, fireman or guard to see the aspect of a signal in a snowstorm as it was in fog. With snow, other platelayers had to be out clearing the snow out of the points pulleys, freeing signals and watching out all the time for passing trains.

In those days the Settle & Carlisle was a very busy line, with shunting movements, branch passenger trains, through expresses, etc. etc. Oh, and could it snow there! In a double emergency like this our gang was called upon to keep the points clear through the day. We did not get the chance during the night for the regular platelayers had the first claim of all overtime on their own length, so they took the jobs that paid off the best. But we did get a little extra payment during the day for working in the snow. On one occasion in 1934 it snowed on and off, day and night, for more than a week. And with some of the men on Fog Signalman's duty and the others full-time clearing snow from the points, signals and rodding, a shortage of manpower arose and an enquiry was made to our gang for temporary Fog Signalmen.

I volunteered and, as I previously knew the extent of their duties, I was hurriedly passed out. Sent home at noon to take a rest, I had to report at the Junction signal-box at 5.30pm, to take orders, and collect my gear. I remember the signalman, George Risely, well, and after a little more briefing I made my way to my fogging post. This was Hawes Junction up distant signal which was situated between the north end of Moorcock Tunnel and Lunds Viaduct. I had to be prepared to stay there until 6.00am. I felt proud to be in sole charge of the various equipment – a set of flags, red, yellow and green – a lighted fully-trimmed hand lamp that would show four different colours by pressing a button and turning the case to the colour required (red, green, amber, or clear) and also several packets of detonators, each holding twelve.

It was very dark and snowing heavily, with a gale of wind that was coming right out of the north, straight from the top of Wild Boar Fell. I was there to time. Just a few words, and my predecessor on the job was gone.

Left by myself, in full charge, I became full of nervous tension and a bit of fear as I thought of the long night in front of me. I had the usual type of fog hut, made of concrete, with an iron brazier and plenty of coal. Luckily for me, the snow was coming to the back of the hut. The poor man fogging the down distant would have the snow blowing right into his face, for these huts had no doors on.

I was situated so that I had a good view of the signal, but at times I could not see it for the whirling snow.

I sat a while . . . the signal was on, so there should be a detonator on the line. My mate had never said anything! I wondered! Better check on it! So I went to examine the rail and found it covered with two inches of snow. I scraped this off for ten yards each side of where the detonators should be, but couldn't find one. So I put one of mine on the line, strapping it down firmly with the clips attached. Then I went back to the hut to warm my numbed hands. Five minutes or so later the signal was lowered, so I hurriedly collected by detonator; a minute or so afterwards a train came thundering past – and banged a detonator off right outside my 'palace', scaring me something awful.

My mate had evidently been too lazy to walk far to put it on. He was all right – he knew how near it was and could sit with his fingers in his ears when a train passed!

I thought I was getting off to a bad start. I could see, when the signal was pulled off, that the snow which had plastered over had not shaken free. So I placed another detonator (fog signals, we called them) on the line, then climbed about twenty rungs up the iron ladder to clean the glasses.

I did not mind putting a detonator on the line after a train had passed, but I was terrified to go and take one off when I saw the signal come off.

Actually, it did not matter so much if an engine did crack one when the signal was off, for if it was a bad night without any visibility it gave the driver a clue where he was. If one was cracked in error, all it did was to slow the train up to a reasonable speed until it had passed all the signals, then it would be away again. But don't try it with any of the Scots expresses, unless there was a good reason, I was told . . .

But there was no object in cracking one when the signal was off, needlessly to slow the train down and so, as soon as the signal did come off, out I rushed to collect my 'banger'. I knew to a yard where it was, but still had to feel for it in the snow.

Just what I was frightened of did actually happen. I was crouched feeling for the detonator, when a train loomed up about ten yards away with his cylinder taps open. I jumped back, curled up like a hedgehog at the side of the line, and the detonator banged off about a yard from me. What a job I had volunteered for!

After that, when I had cause to remove one from the rail I brushed it off with my flag stick; someone would find them when the snow cleared.

Around midnight I was getting a little scared of the snow and the darkness and all the trains coming in their stocking feet. I couldn't hear them until they almost came into sight. I dare not relax, or miss a train. If they were occupying the main line at the station, I might cause an accident. Also, I was feeling spooky. I remembered a man had been killed on the line near my end of the tunnel a few years before. These thoughts didn't help. I was wishing 6.00am would soon arrive.

But salvation was in sight at about three o'clock. The wind dropped, it stopped snowing, and soon afterwards the stars came out. In about another half hour the distant signal started showing on/off – on/off several times. This was the recognised system for the signalman to call his Fog Signalmen in when he no longer required them.

It would be well towards 6.00am when I got home to bed, after walking back to the box with my gear and cracking a bit with George and the down distant fellow, a chap called Mason.

I felt quite a man – I had earned some extra money as overtime rate, and with nine hours off for rest I wouldn't have to go to work that day, and would get a day's wage for it also. That was the last time I was called upon to do that particular duty, but in the years that followed I many times called out and instructed men to go out and protect the signals I was in charge of. That winter, it seems to me now, was a very cold one. We had lots of snow and frost . . . and believe me, it could freeze up all around Hawes Junction.

The water troughs there, as far as I can recollect, were about half way between the station and Rise Hill Tunnel, but maybe a little nearer to the tunnel. During frosty weather they were steam-heated from a coal-fired boiler on the up side to keep them from freezing. Steam raisers from Hellifield shed used to man the boiler during these periods.

But in really hard frost like we were having then, the boiler couldn't cope, so our gang was diverted to the troughs to keep them open so that engines could still get their water at speed.

We would rake the ice off the water. This was nothing – it was the ice that formed on the rail and sleepers that was the problem. As each engine picked up water at speed it splashed all around, and was immediately frozen hard. We had to pick and shovel this off, or it would have built up so high it would not have been safe for the trains to run on.

All the railway for over a mile in each direction was a huge sheet of ice on both lines, over the sleeper end, on the cess or path at the side, inches thick and almost impossible to walk on. The ground on the down line side of the track sloped down to a field wall, and this side was just one slope of ice. One slip and a man could slide for yards. As usual, it was my lot to be allocated to that side of the line to do the chipping and picking. Ganger Joe and his best men chose the up line, which was much safer to walk on.

We all wore clogs in those days. I could never really walk properly in these, let alone stand and work on the side of a sloping ice-field.

I would be busy at this job of chipping and picking, when our lookout man would blow his horn and shout, "Train just leaving tunnel."

There it was coming . . . the whistle blowing . . . the driver lowering his scoop to pick up water. We would just scramble clear, watching carefully that we didn't skate down the bank, then the train was on us. Swoosh and it was past, the engine scattering more water over us, putting another layer of ice on top of the stuff we were hacking off. After leaving the troughs, there was a trail of ice almost to the station, through it being scattered from under the train. On the up line this occurred again, almost to the tunnel end.

What I was most afraid of, apart from that slide down into Garsdale Valley, was a tank lid on top of the tender flying off and hitting one of us. These lids, similar to a heavy pan lid, were made of strong steel perhaps twenty inches in diameter, and were – in theory – chained to the tender so that they would not fall off. But if the train was going at a fast speed the water must have been filling the tender at a terrible pressure, and if the lid was not in place I have seen the water fly out high into the air, soaking anyone who may have been working on the line nearby. If the tender lid was in place and the driver did not raise his scoop soon enough the force of water inside would knock the lid off forcibly, often breaking the chain so that the lid would go bounding off the side. None broke loose whilst we were on ice-breaking duties, but I knew it did happen frequently towards the trailing ends of the troughs. And to prove it, if anyone cares to look, there will still be several lying rusting down the bank near each end of the troughs' former site.

With the problems of clearing the ice from those troughs on my mind, I used to have nightmares in my sleep. At times I could see the ice building up so thick in front and behind me that I couldn't cope with it. In my sleep I could see the expresses getting so high on the rail that they would topple over and slide down into the valley . . .

Ted Wilson, the ganger on this length, told us one of his men had slipped on the ice there some years before and fallen squarely on his back in one of the troughs just as a train was leaving the tunnel, and was only just pulled clear in the nick of time. That made me think! I was long and narrow – I mustn't fall in or I might drown!

They told me about another man a long while ago. A very tiny man who fell lengthways in the trough on the down line. Before anyone could get him out he was scooped up with the water into the engine tender and was only seen again for a few seconds. Passing Mallerstang signal-box, the driver glanced into his water gauge glass and saw a face inside, and by the way the lips were moving it was trying to tell him something. Then there was nothing. The tiny figure had passed through into the boiler, perhaps to escape amongst the steam . . .

At about this time there was a big reorganisation scheme under way at Leeds City station, concerning the layout of the sidings and platforms, the station buildings, and the railway-owned Queens Hotel.

All the demolition materials came to Hawes Junction to be dumped, with special train-loads or part of a load arriving daily for weeks and weeks. We constructed a small siding for about sixteen wagons, alongside the branch line, with a good drop into the bottom for the wagons which had to be emptied by hand. It was christened the 'Muck Bank'.

Load after load of good quality dressed walling stone went down that bank – Yorkshire Shoddies, they were. Many a wagon load of good timber went down also, some of it to be burned in huge bonfires. In addition, spent ballast and other waste materials came from Nottingham, Leicester, Cudworth and other old Midland stations being re-built. When the edge of the tip got too far from the wagons comfortably to unload, we spent Saturday mornings slewing the road to the edge of the tip.

I am not sure when the landslide occurred in Shale Cutting at Dent – 1935, I would think. We were working there at the time, digging a deep drain around the crest of the cutting. There was a lot of seepage during a wet time into the cutting from Wold Fell higher up and the small cut round the top was made up. We were putting in twelve-inch pipes to collect the water and take it down each side into the new drains we had laid. Twelve-inch pipes need a big hole, and we were dropping them in all of four feet deep.

There had been two or three rainy days. The day of the landslide it rained all day really heavy, and was too wet for us to walk to Dent Head.

We spent the day in the big Storm Cabin at Dent station, some sleeping or playing games. I spent the time just listening to the Dent lads – Charlie Campbell, Jack Sutton, Frank Sedgewick and Tommy Capstick. At 4.30pm Ganger Jack Aikrigg of Dent Head length came rushing up to the signalman shouting, "Stop the job. The whole of the top side of Shale Cutting is slipping and is touching the outside rail of the up line and moving the aqueduct." Our cabin was right behind the signal box, so we heard all this.

All traffic was stopped at the Junction and Blea Moor, whilst flagmen were sent out immediately to protect the obstruction from both sides. Luckily both sections were clear of trains when the landslide happened. However, there was no train to get us back to our home station and it was almost dark and raining heavily.

"Come on lads," our Ganger said briskly, "We will walk home. There's no rain in the tunnel." I remember old 'Wem', who lodged with Joe, muttering. "Thinks we are as daft as his bloody Gurkhas!" . . . But we had the doubtful consolation that we would meet no trains, at least.

We were called out again around 9.30pm to be picked up by the Carlisle ballast train, with some of the senior officers of the Engineering Department, plus Appleby Relay Gang. The Special Engineer and his Assistant, from Leeds, came in from the other end in the Engineers' Saloon (or 'Nanny Cart' as it was called).

But there was nothing we could do; too much rain, and shale slowly creeping along. We only had fog lamps to see by. I think the height of the cutting at that point would be easily a hundred feet, if not more. From then on it was a big job. Trains of low-sided ballast wagons were called in, and there were hundreds of men on the job, shovelling into them day and night. There were gangs from Appleby, Carlisle, Skipton, Shipley, Leeds, Blackburn, Preston, and all the platelayers for fifty miles around. The scene very much put me in mind of the early pictures I had seen of navvies building the railways.

For a while our gang was busy at home, emptying down our new muck bank. It couldn't have been better placed for this emergency.

I don't remember how long the line was closed, or if single-line working was in operation for trains over the down line, but I know the P.W. Dept, had full use of the up line for some weeks.

Eventually a contract was let out to an outside civil contracting firm to further lighten the slip and put in a big concrete retaining wall at the foot of the bank. A special train was made up for the contractors, with a number of wagons for aggregate and cement, timber for shuttering, the largest concrete mixer I had seen up to that time, and platforms for the men to work on. There was a special cooking van, and another for the men to eat and rest in. All this topped up with a guard's van – but not a toilet on the whole site!

The train was made up each night at Settle with more materials, most of the workers being Settle men who travelled with the train in the morning to work, and home with it at night.

Eventually the slip was boxed in and made safe. During the time we worked on it, this became known as "The Big Slip' and has been called this ever since. We worked there a long time after the contractors had finished; we tidied up, put the new drain around the top and a new one the length of the cutting on the up side.

The 'Nanny Cart' stopped for ten minutes each fortnight with us. Towards the end of our work one very wet day, we were all in the cabin and heard the conversation between our Ganger and the Chief Engineer from Leeds. I remember the latter saying to Joe, "The rain is incessant!" It was the first time I and most of the gang had heard the word – we often laughed about it. It was a word not used much in that area, I think. They continued to talk together and the Chief said, "Well, Gamsby, I think we have got that landslide beaten and made safe." Joe agreed with him.

Then me, ignorant me, piped up from the back of the cabin, "Yes, it has been cured, but don't you think it wouldn't have happened if we hadn't dug that big ditch round the top?"

Silence fell for a moment, then their conversation went on as though no one had spoken. When the Engineer had gone, Joe stood up and swore at me for being such an ignorant fool. I think the people in Dent town could have heard my mates laughing at me. When Joe had finished swearing, the Dent Ganger, Charlie Campbell, got to his feet to reprimand him. Charlie was a good-living, religious man, and he said, "Joe Gamsby, if the Lord struck you down now for swearing at that lad as you have done, it would just serve you right." Joe turned to give Charlie a mouthful of the same

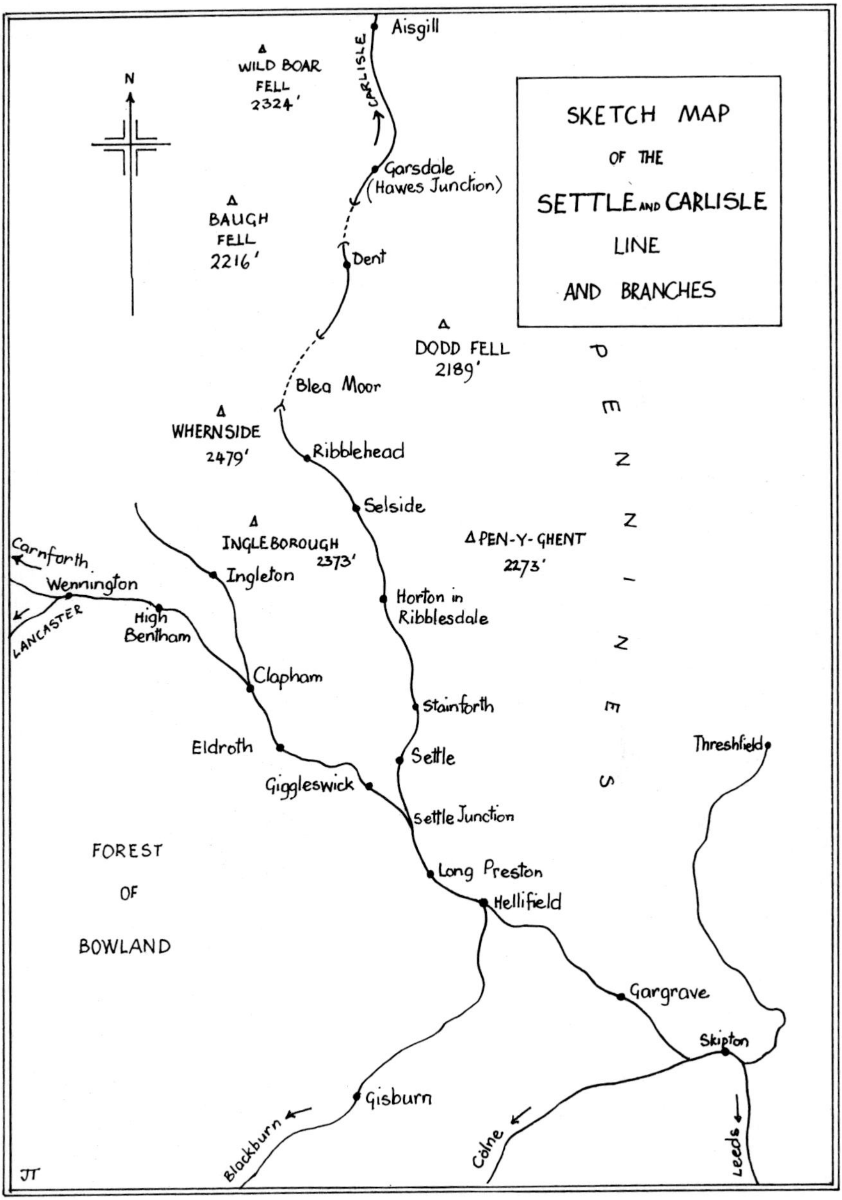
SKETCH MAP
OF THE
SETTLE AND CARLISLE
LINE
AND BRANCHES
N
WILD BOAR
FELL
2324'
BAUGH
FELL
2216'
DODD FELL
2189'
WHERNSIDE
2479'
INGLEBOROUGH
2373'
PEN-Y-GHENT
2273'
PENNINES
FOREST
OF
BOWLAND
CARLISLE
Aisgill
Garsdale
(Hawes Junction)
Dent
Blea Moor
Ribblehead
Selside
Horton in
Ribblesdale
Stainforth
Settle
Settle Junction
Long Preston
Hellifield
Gargrave
Skipton
Threshfield
Carnforth
Wennington
LANCASTER
High
Bentham
Ingleton
Clapham
Eldroth
Giggleswick
Gisburn
Blackburn
Colne
Leeds
JT

and nearly choked – his false teeth had broken into two pieces. What a laugh went up then . . .

But that Big Slip had broken off at the top just where we had cut that semi-circle; nothing had stirred higher up.

For some time I had been thinking of asking for a transfer out of the P.W. into the Traffic Department. I would have liked to be a locomotive fireman, but had missed my chance owing to my age.

Whilst working on the Big Slip I had come into contact with goods guards from Carlisle, Skipton, and Hellifield. I fancied their job, riding about the countryside, enjoying the varied scenery of town and country – and getting paid for it. They told me there were plenty of vacancies in their Department, so I decided to apply.

CHAPTER TWO

Out and About in the Brake-van

MY APPLICATION for a transfer to the Traffic Department was duly made and on 8 June 1936 I was appointed to be a porter at Hellifield station and transferred there the same day. As it was impossible to jump into a guard's job right away, I would have to go through various grades of shunter; but I was on the first step, as a porter. To progress to the position of guard through these various steps could take years, but I was young enough to do that.

What a busy station Hellifield was in those days. In summer, amongst the regular express and other passengers trains, there would be crammed in, some weekends, from sixteen to twenty excursion trains from Leeds, Bradford, Sheffield, and other towns on the route. These were mostly going to Morecambe, with others to Windermere (Lakeside) via Carnforth and the Furness line. They were mostly 'run-throughs'. Some were booked to stop ten minutes to take on water. Sometimes a non-corridor train would stop for toilet purposes – what a scamper that was! We had an 'Eldorado' ice-cream vendor on the station; he did well with those trains. He got so carried away with his selling capabilities he would get onto the trains carrying about 100 wafers, and he would forget the stop was only for water or picking-up. Several times the carriage doors were slammed shut and he was carried through to the next stop, which would be Morecambe.

One week in six I would be the station signal lampman, bringing in and trimming all the main line signals, overhead shunting signals and ground signals, at Hellifield North and South junctions and the Lankey Box (L. &

Y.) and also the intermediate block at Otterburn. This was a pretty rough job, especially in rain and snow, but worse still if it was windy, for the lamps had the habit of waiting until one had climbed thirty to forty signal steps, then they would blow out. So down we had to come and try all over again. We would perhaps climb from fifteen to twenty signals in a day. I used to think, if they were all put end to end in one climb, I should be able to peep through a man-hole into Heaven . . .

I hated every minute of the porter's position, but had to stick it if I was to get on. I had never been used to wearing a clean shirt and a tie or having to clean my boots every day. And I bungled many jobs with my awkwardness.

I had a mate who started at Hellifield the same day as I did – Bill Bullock – who was a man similar in ways to myself. We also had a station foreman called Alec Kirkside getting on for retirement; born and reared on a farm at Hawes, blunt of speech and to the point, but very honest.

He stood a while one day, watching Dick and me trying to post some wonderful coloured L.M.S. posters on a billboard. "Give over lads!" he said "I think you would be doing more good if you went and helped John Winter in the hayfield." I would rather have been there too!

Hellifield sidings at that time were very busy with the continuous clatter-bang-bang of wagons being shunted and made up into their respective trains. Working around the station, day and night, were High Level Shunt engine, Low Level Trip engine, Passenger Shunt engine, Loco Coal Stage engine, Cattle Dock Shunt engine and on five days each week the Hellifield Dump engine. Most of these engines worked round the clock on a continuous rota, and amongst it all the regular passenger trains were attaching or detaching horse boxes, special cattle, fish and other passenger train stock. Some thirty or more freight trains in each twenty-four hours attached or detached traffic in the sidings. Several were made up there each day for Blackburn, Lostock Hall, Springs Branch, Rose Grove, Agecroft . . . and many more places. There were also as many made up for Carlisle and beyond.

The different routing whistles of all these shunt engines and train engines were worth listening to. The signalmen at Hellifield knew every one, and signalled them forward accordingly. I knew what most of the whistles meant and still remember some.

We also had another unofficial set of whistles at Hellifield. The village is grouped around the station and at this period I would think one-third of the population were loco men – drivers and firemen, with one guard on average to each set of these. Most of those drivers had their own special whistle. When backed up and leaving, down the Lankey, it was their little message to their wives. When arriving back, at any time during the day or night, from a journey, as they got within a quarter of a mile or so away from the station they would send their message. Each woman knew her husband's poppety-pop, and could begin to make breakfast, tea, or supper, whichever fitted the time of day. The fireman's wife and the guard's wife would know too that it was also their man's train.

The only time I was a hero was at Hellifield; but only a temporary hero, I admit. We had two down expresses in the afternoons, the St. Pancras to Glasgow and the St. Pancras to Edinburgh. I don't recall which of these trains was involved in the episode. I was standing well down at the north end of the platform, which was for my allocated portion of the train and the guard had waved his green flag for it to proceed. As it was gathering speed and passing by me I noticed an unusually large gap between two carriages about the middle of the train. I started to run with it, in order to see what was wrong, and saw that the coupling had broken and was trailing on permanent way. The rear portion of the train was being pulled along by the connected gangway, the steam heating and vacuum pipes and the electric light connections, all of which were fully stretched out. I immediately threw my arms up in the air as an alarm stop signal and gave a terrible shout at the guard as he was passing me with his head out of the window. Without hesitation he applied the vacuum brake and brought the train to a standstill outside Hellifield North Junction box. It was just as well the brakes took hold at the front of the train simultaneously with the back, or it would have broken the train in two.

The train was well behind schedule when leaving Hellifield, for the passengers had to be distributed about the train, the faulty coach detached and the rear portion coupled up again. This is where the passenger shunt engine came into use to do the work from the rear. The delay would be put down as 'well intentioned' or 'justified'.

Later that day I was called into the Station-master's Office, where also was the Chief Controller from Skipton, who had made the journey especially to congratulate me on my observance and the speed with which I went into action to stop the train. It probably saved the signalmen somewhere along the line a nasty affair and perhaps an accident if it had divided as speed. Certainly if anyone had been passing through the gangway at the time, it could have been the end of them.

Being a porter, I met a great number of people, including various lords and ladies travelling from the old L. & Y. and changing from Liverpool or Manchester trains into the Scots express for their holidays north of the Border. Just before 12 August we would get a lot of this type of traveller going north for grouse shooting or salmon fishing. They were accompanied by gamekeepers, valets, servants, dogs, and all the paraphernalia that they thought they would need – shooting sticks, rods, guns, hampers, and other luggage by the ton. What they carried with them must have been big business for the Railway Company – it certainly was for us porters; in one of those weeks I received no less than £12 in tips.

By far the people I liked to meet the most were the large numbers of railwaymen who used to gather in the porters' room at Hellifield. This room was large and clean, with gas oven and rings for boiling the kettle, and a coal stove whenever the fire was needed. Guards, ticket collectors, drivers and firemen, wagon tappers and other grades used to make for this friendly place. The trainmen, after being relieved of their trains, had perhaps an hour or maybe many hours sometimes to wait for their return workings. They could have a brew-up with their 'snap'. At times there would be men from as far away as Carlisle, Polmadie, Leeds, Barrow, Carnforth, Skipton, Bolton, Salford, Agecroft, Lostock Hall, Wigan, Rose Grove and other places. The different dialects were wonderful to listen to. It was here I heard my first Lancashire dialect from some of those down to earth 'Lankey' men from Blackburn and Bowton – not to forget the strong robust dialect of the Carlisle men.

I did a great variety of jobs at Hellifield – some good, some not so good. The others or I were often called upon to do a bit of carriage shunting if the regular shunters were not at hand. This was making up trains of various stock, attaching and detaching horse boxes or coaches from one train to another. There were three full-time passenger shunters working a continuous rota between them, and even they could not be in two places at once. It was a dirty greasy job; this was the way of it . . .

> Make sure the train had come to a stand. Slide down from the platform. Duck under the buffers. Shout 'Ease up' to the driver if he hadn't already, to take the tension from the couplings. Disconnect the vacuum pipe so that train or engine could not move in any way. Pull the two electric plugs apart, placing their ends in the boxes provided at the ends of the carriage to stop them swinging about. Turn off the steam heater taps and disconnect their jointing brackets and pin them securely on their out of action brackets. Then unscrew the coupling sufficiently to be able to lift the shackle off the hook. Hang it on the bracket provided

for it when not in use, so that it was not dangling loose under the vehicle. Then, finally, before getting out from under, we connected and pinned the vacuum pipe to its stopper, making sure it was not sucking air when the driver wished to blow his brakes off. If the train was a corridor train we had to divide, we would do this first, then fit a board at each end so that nobody accidentally walked out of the end of the train.

All this had to be done in under two minutes; a man was reckoned to be very slow if he took longer than that. I was once well beaten, trying to uncouple a coach from the down 'Waverley'. I simply had no idea how. Several others tried but still we couldn't. Then the guard of the train got down and did it for us. He was one of the posh passenger guards, done up in gold braid, but not too proud to get down in an emergency. Simple, it was a buck-eye coupling!

The passenger shunter's was a horrible job if it was raining because the guttering that ran along the side of the coach roof drained down at the ends like running taps on top of him, and all the time he had to be on the alert for any movement of the train if it happened to stop with all buffers compressed. It was one heck of a job without a doubt. I had to take over for a short period one wild winter's morning. A terrible gale was blowing and it blew some of the carriage siding roof off. Frankie Farthing was on night passenger shunt duty and was riding on the step of an empty passenger train coming out of the sidings when part of an iron stanchion knocked him off and he was killed.

After a while, at my own wish, I was passed out as a temporary porter guard, and I got some nice little jobs. If a passenger guard failed to turn up for duty, or for some other reason a guard was required and there were no others available, I was hurriedly put on the job. First, though, I had several weeks riding about with the regular guards to familiarise myself with the routes; 'learning the road' it was called. How lovely it was this training – riding to and from Leeds, Carlisle, Blackburn, Carnforth, Morecambe – learning the rules and getting good advice.

One of our regular guards was off sick for a long time. He was Dick Oldfield, and I started covering for him full-time. What an enjoyable summer I had! But I was told, almost weekly, by someone or other, "Don't get too clever, you are only a common porter."

Then, in the Autumn the Station Master asked me if I would take a position as temporary goods guard, to cover holidays, sickness, or emergency. I was only too glad to agree for this was the reason I had come to Hellifield, and to be a temporary guard, so early in my service, was better than having to wait many years to be a permanent one.

I was appointed temporary goods guard at Hellifield on 15 June 1937 and started learning 'roads' in earnest. I had a good knowledge over a large area of the main line by now, but the new job was more exacting. I had to learn the layout of sidings and their holding capacity, so I spent a lot of time with the local shunting freights; Skipton, Carlisle Pickup, Lime, Hawes Pickup, Ingleton, also away down the 'Lankey' and on many of its off-shoots. It wasn't long before I could rhyme off all stations between Carlisle and Leeds, Hellifield and Morecambe, Carnforth and Barrow, Hellifield to Manchester . . . Oh, shut up, Dick . . .!

It wasn't so bad when arriving at large sidings, for there was a shunter in charge and by the time I got to the front of the train they had hooked their wagons off and started shunting . . . and they knew just where they wanted everything. I would have been absolutely lost if I had to shunt Settle, Stainforth, Horton or Hawes without these men, but had to do the smaller stations with the help of a porter. But normal putting-off or picking-up during the night-time was done by the guard, excepting in the larger places with their marshalling yards.

I was very soon sent off for a train on my own. This first job was a very easy one, but even then I was filled with apprehension until it was time to go off duty.

I had to sign on at 7.00pm to go to Heysham Harbour for a cattle train, a light engine with driver and fireman coming off the shed at 7.15pm to go for this. I could please myself; either I could ride on the engine with them or go passenger on the Morecambe train then about due. On this first occasion I chose to go on the engine, and stick with my mates – Bill Deakin (driver), and I forget the other.

Down to Morecambe first, then half-way round the triangle, then tender-first to Heysham where the signalman put us straight onto our train. Twenty-two wagons and the brake; four at the front, fully fitted. Express freight headlights on the engine; lamps trimmed and lighted; fire going in the brake van. We were away by 10pm.

Coming up past Bentham my confidence began to return. Nothing to it! We got safely off the Old Road, detached some cattle at Hellifield and again at Whalley, Blackburn, Bolton. I was always, afterwards, glad of the shunter's help at Bolton for I never did figure out where their cattle dock was. We finished with the few wagons that we had left at Windsor Bridge, arriving back at Hellifield between 5.00 and 6.00am. In fact, we should have finished with the train at Blackburn, but the forward workings had broken down and we had to go through with them.

A few more jobs and I soon gained in confidence and still got plenty of passenger workings amongst my jobs, for goods guards stepped into the vacancies on a temporary arrangement. Dick Oldfield was still off sick, so I was covering his job again for a while. One of these was to Carlisle with an express – out of Hellifield about 11.20, work it through to Carlisle, express back to Leeds with the same Leeds engine men I went down with in the morning, then work the down Leeds – Morecambe stopping train to Hellifield, relieved there by a Morecambe guard.

Another job that came around at times was working a stopping passenger train from Hellifield to Manchester and back, using the same engine for the round trip.

Another trip I liked very much was working the Yorkshire Post to Carnforth, leaving Hellifield at 2.20 or 2.30am. Usually there were two coaches in front for the odd passenger, and conveyed to Carnforth regularly to balance passenger train workings from there. To the rear of these were three loaded vans, one almost full of Yorkshire Post newspapers, another full with mail-bags, and the third one loaded with general parcels or fish in boxes. I had no work in these vans; they were sorted and arranged when loaded at Leeds. We would arrive at Carnforth around 3.15am. There would be a short period of time when there would be nothing to do in Carnforth and we would be booked to assist on the First Mail out of Euston as far as Millom with stops at Grange, Ulverston, Barrow and Millom.

Whilst at Carnforth the Second Mail would fly through on its journey north into Scotland, and on the odd occasion I caught a glimpse, through the windows, of the G.P.O. sorters busy amongst the mail, pitching letters into different pigeon holes. We had a van on our train, and at different points they used to sling out a mail-bag into the apparatus on the line side which used to catch it.

I was usually shoved into the newspaper van on leaving Carnforth to get them ready by the door – first stations first. It was a hot and dirty job; the newsprint would come off on your hands and clothes, whilst the bundles still held so much heat in them from the presses it was uncomfortable to sit on them! One thing I noticed about the newspaper suppliers; they put quite a number of loose ones in for any staff who cared to take a copy.

We would arrive at Millom just after six o'clock. This was a great treat for me because it was not so many years before that I had left that district.

This was where I was born and brought up as a boy.

I had one memorable episode at Barrow-in-Furness when working that First Mail. We carried vast quantities of Lyons cakes, in cartons perhaps twenty inches square. The Carnforth passenger guards, who had worked the train from London, had the cakes sorted into their respective heaps, handy for their stations. After Ulverston I pushed a heap of 'Barrow cakes' to the door for handiness. At Barrow I was handing out the cartons two at a time for the porters to pack on a barrow, and in doing so several chocolate Swiss rolls fell out onto the platform. There was always an L.M.S. policeman on hand for that train, and the station foreman on duty that morning was a holy terror both to staff and passengers.

Both these worthies stepped up and took hold of the bottom box, turned it over, and there was a neat piece cut out of the bottom, just the right size for a roll to drop through. They opened the box, counted the contents and found two missing – whereupon they grabbed me, my traps and lunch bag, and rushed me into an office, a porter guard being put on the train to cover my workings to Millom. A senior police officer from the town was there within a few minutes, and I was subjected to one solid hour of abuse and victimisation. My baggage was searched, and they even examined my teeth to look for traces of Swiss roll. And all the time that bully of a station foreman shouted abuse at me; he would, in fact, have liked to torture me to extract a confession.

I was innocent, so I really had nothing to fear. I was set free in time to take up my working back to Hellifield where I wrote out a full report of what had happened at Barrow.

I heard no more about the incident, but I was still very sore and angry. I knew where the Swiss rolls had gone all right, for when I took over from the passenger guard at Carnforth he had just eaten some. I recalled seeing the cream and crumbs on his lips, but didn't think anything about it at the time.

Apparently there was a lot of pilfering going on with the train, and a close watch was being kept.

Maybe six weeks after this event I was on the Mail Train to Millom again and was still rankling about the affair. I started handing out the parcels . . . the same porters . . the same policeman . . . and the same station foreman.

Upon seeing me he bawled out, "Here he is again. It is funny, we haven't lost any cakes since we took him in." Famous last words! I sprang out of the van door, landed him one on his chin, another around about his belly button . . . and as he went over amongst the cakes I gave him a hefty one under his sit-upon with my right shoe. By now the merchandise and papers were out. A Barrow guard standing by said, "You had better be going, lad!" So I signalled the train away, sharp.

At Barrow, on my return, the station-master was on duty. He looked at me in a very serious way. No station foreman! The railway policeman was there and I am sure to this day he was trying his best not to grin. Most of the station staff seemed to be around on the platform when my train drew up, and it was plain to see they were pleased about something.

The station-master was waiting for me on the platform when I arrived at Hellifield – by the look on his face I could tell that someone from Barrow-in-Furness had been on the phone to him about me. I still hadn't cooled down properly, and from the minute I had landed one on the foreman I was sure it would be instant dismissal when I reached my home station. I remember how he tried to look serious as he reprimanded me, and ended by saying, "Leave it with me."

I think it was the injustice that I had been subjected to at Barrow on the previous trip and the reputation of the station foreman that had got me off. I heard, soon after that, that the latter had had a good beating-up by a passenger he had been tongue-lashing. He will have passed on by now; if he hasn't he will be over 100, so I forgive him. But I was never allowed to work that train again.

I saw a lot of places I would never have seen if I hadn't taken that job. For instance, work a special train to Manchester, and I would get a free ticket into Belle Vue Circus and Zoo. Or if I took a special Football train to Blackburn, I would get a free ticket to the match. But I usually chose to wander about the streets of the towns; all was so new to me after never having being far from my little home village perched on a hill in Cumberland. Many times I went passenger to Rochdale to work a Rochdale-Hellifield freight back. This was a nice little job – a fast booked train with only about sixteen wagons back to Hellifield non-stop. I liked this trip, but I dreaded working a train through Bury Hollow, though with a short train such as this I had no need to worry.

There was some kind of sharp dip in the line between Bury and Bolton which caused a lot of trains to divide and caused a lot of havoc, especially with coal trains. There was some sort of safety device in the hollow to protect the guard and his portion of train, should he become divided accidentally.

I worked several times around Horwich Fork and Horwich and once went to the loco shed there with my driver and fireman to collect a light engine to pick up a train from Bolton. I worked many empty van and wagon trains into Manchester Ship Canal docks and Salford. There was always a shout for vans when an extra large cargo of bananas came in. I remember being propelled brake-first underneath Manchester, through a tunnel to open out within sight of ships loading and unloading. And me in a goods brake leading the way, with may-be twenty-five wagons pushing me towards the water with the engine still in the tunnel!

One place we used to propel down into, I think, was Salford. It was so steep going into that dungeon of a goods yard that the shunter used to push a huge wooden chock through each wagon wheel to lock it so that we did not get out of control.

I was then about at the top of my career as a 'Nig-Nog', a word that was in popular use at that time. It seemed a fitting description of a young, awkward, temporary guard. And a locomotive passed-cleaner also came into this category – a name invented by the old hands. We were called it pretty often.

I was well qualified to be called a 'Nig-Nog', the amount of lumber I got into. Still, with the advantage of being one, lots of miscalculations were overlooked.

I have started off with a train which had an old hand for a driver and a passed cleaner for a fireman, and heard the driver say to a shunter or someone. "What have I done to deserve this. I have a Nig-Nog for a fireman, and another riding behind!"

But the Hellifield drivers and guards were a grand lot and would be most helpful at all times. And the word 'Nig-Nog' was mostly used in an affectionate and friendly manner.

We had two sections of loco men at Hellifield. Some were the old Lancashire & Yorkshire men and had always worked on that section. Come the closing of the old L. & Y. shed there, they were transferred to the former Midland shed. The other section comprised regular Midland men. Each clung to and praised the particular section to which they belonged.

I personally thought the L. & Y. men the most helpful. Though they intermixed and were together in the train-working rosters, they preferred to work over their old sections when possible and even used to change turns to get back onto their favourite routes.

What a busy place Hellifield was then, and how interesting. I regret I cannot quote now how many sets of loco men and guards worked trains in and out of that station in each twenty-four hours.

Hawes Junction (Garsdale) station in the 1920s, looking north, and its signalbox. The branch down the valley to Hawes is on the right, the main lines to and from Carlisle on the left. Pilot engines which had assisted up or down trains were detached here in former days and at one time it was a busy location.

At that time there were numerous heavy coal trains running between the Nottinghamshire or Yorkshire coalfields, all passing through Skipton and Hellifield on to Carnforth and Lancaster, and as many empty wagons trains returning to be loaded again. Some of these trains carried seventy loaded wagons, or seventy empties.

We had no coal train workings on Hellifield rotas. Only the old regulars could manage these trains over the various gradients and dips in the line. Carnforth and Barrow men were good, being born to the road. Skipton and Leeds men were as good – as they had to be when you saw a double-headed coal train with seventy loose-coupled wagons loaded with coal flying through Hellifield to get a run at Giggleswick bank.

They would keep the couplings tight on passing Settle Junction box, so that all were stretched out through the dip before they got into the bank in earnest. And the guard's brake, on the back of the train, was pulled along like an empty salmon tin dangling on a string. Whatever he did, he would have no impression on the train there. I have known quite a few break loose on that little bit between the Junction starting signal and Giggleswick down distant signal, but never anything really serious.

If the couplings were allowed to become slack through any dip, they would probably take hold with a bad snatch when tightening up and a break-loose could easily happen. Often there would be quite a nasty dip under some of the over bridges. The P.W. Dept. were frequently lifting sections of track to make a better bed for the sleepers, but the height of some of the bridges did not always allow this and so they ran the 'lift'out before they reached the bridges, then took it up gradually on the other side. This method left some of the dips which I have previously mentioned. Others were a natural down and then an up gradient, as at Settle Junction. But I can name several bridges over the sections on which I worked where great care had to be used when working loose-coupled trains. The ups and downs were the same on the up line also, but were never so treacherous to empty wagon trains; they had no weight to shove and pull.

The worst 'train divide' I know happened right beside Arkholme signal box when I was working the Yorkshire Post to Carnforth and the 10.30am express back. For most of one week, single line working was in operation around the obstacles. A dozen or more wagons and their contents were scattered on the hedge and in the field right by the box.

The train had somehow broken a coupling – a snatch, I suppose. A gap had arisen between the front and back portion and this had widened out. Then the rear portion had caught up with the front portion and over-run it. It was possibly the worst scattering I had seen, although I saw a beauty some time later at Rose Grove.

So – imagine my feelings, one Monday morning, with several inches of snow on the ground and after a week-end of hard frost, when I was told to join two light engines coming off the shed at 7.30am, and travel to Settle Junction with them to attach to a coal train of seventy wagons before taking them to Carnforth. Although I had trained the Carnforth road with other guards, I had not worked a goods train over the section; and now I had to work a double-headed one at that, with that terrible seventy. This, after all, was a section of line that only professionals were allowed to work. And to make matters worse, my two loco men were a pair of young passed firemen.

It took some time to get round seventy wagons in two roads to see that all was safe: no brakes pinned or rubbing, all couplings safe, all wagon doors secure. I found particulars of the train in the brake-van, for it was the custom of all guards leaving a train in a siding to leave a journal ready for the next man.

The signalman turned the two engines (Midland 3F 0–6–0s) into the road to attach the first pick up. When I was satisfied all was ready to be moved, and the signalman gave us the dummy, my enginemen drew out into the main Giggleswick line clear of the sidings, and then backed gently onto the rear half which I hooked on. I then hurried back to my van, slackened off the handbrake and gave the lads in front the 'right-away' signal. Nine o'clock . . . it had already taken us an hour. There was a pop from both engines. We were about to leave! The drivers had several tries to get the train started and eventually we set off . . . but so slowly. I could see quite a few wagon wheels skidding on the rails not far in front of my van. The drivers tried to get a run through the dip to help surmount Gigg bank, but it was as much as they could do to keep the train moving.

We had a lot of the old fat type of axle boxes as well as the more modern oil boxes which all had accumulated water which was now frozen solid. If they would all start turning, and warm up, the ice would melt before we got into the bank. We were only going slow past Giggleswick box and the worst part of the gradient was still in front of us.

I could see the signalman in there, bouncing about in the box, waving and pointing. I could do nothing but look glumly back at him. We might make it if the engines did not start slipping, but if one of them did then this would put more strain on the other; thereupon that also would start to slip and we would be beaten. Also, if one of our inexperienced drivers touched the regulator a fraction more than necessary it would start us off.

I was about two hundred yards past the down starting signal when one started slipping . . . then the other . . . and we came to a stop. I thought we had done well to get this far as I put my brake on hard to stop any movement backwards.

Then they would try again, and I had to let the brake off sharply. We would get only a few yards, before the engines would slip to a stop again. And once again it was on with the brake. The engines would ease back so that all the couplings were compressed and pushing back on the brake.

The compression on seventy wagons, each with two sets of buffers and springs, was considerable – quite a few yards in fact. Often enough this would almost push the engines forward and give them a good start if the two drivers could time their forward movements simultaneously. I had to listen carefully and, just as the tension was being liberated wagon by wagon, I had, upon its reaching me, to let the brake off sharply so that we could be caught on the forward thrust. We tried this many times but it wouldn't work, as we were sadly overloaded or underpowered, or both.

Both firemen meanwhile were down on the permanent way shovelling cinders and ballast on the rail in order to help the driving-wheels to grip. That was no use either.

We had struggled forward fifty yards, but were not yet on the steepest part of the bank. Just then I spotted one of the firemen walking down the off-side of the train to me. The signalman had been out on the platform of his box several times, shouting and waving his arms, but I could not hear what he was saying and, besides, I dare not leave the brake in case the lads in front got the train moving.

I did, however, see a down Morecambe passenger train arrive at the Giggleswick home signal. I estimated the time to be about 10.10am. The fireman said they had decided to divide the train and work half the wagons to Clapham, then return on the wrong line for the back half. He asked that I issue him with a Wrong Line Order, duly signed, to enable them to set back onto the train from Eldroth. This I did. They were soon hooked off and over the top. I then went back to Giggleswick signal box to protect my train. And didn't I cop it off the signalman there, and from Skipton Control.

Apparently, in cases like this in the past, when another train had arrived at Giggleswick behind the one that had stalled, the engine of the second one had unhooked from its train, entered the section gently and helped to push the train over the top. The second loco had then reversed back to its own train under a W.L.O. from the signalman. If we had only known – it would have been simple. But my front end would be nearly at Clapham by then. If only they had sent someone to tell us of the arrangement. It was no use shouting at me!

My two engines eventually arrived back and were hooked on. I joined my train and we made our way to Clapham and into another empty siding. The time was then about 12 noon. The passenger closely followed us to Clapham, and it in turn was closely followed by the noon train to Morecambe. We had to stay inside until the Ingleton branch passenger left, then had to draw out twice to couple our train together again, then back off the branch line onto the down Morecambe line and away. My enginemen took no chances on the down gradient to Wennington with that heavy train, for by now the oil and fat boxes had warmed up and were free and the train would take some holding if the signals happened to be on at Bentham. I was taking no chances either; I had the brake hard on all the way down.

We crawled through Wennington and onto the Carnforth branch. I could hear the two engines gently taking up the slack as they entered the tunnel and just as gently I let off my brake. Going through Melling the lads in front were letting into them, to romp through the dip at Arkholme and up the bank. Somehow, I miscalculated there. I did not feel anything as we went through the dip, but the enginemen told me when we got to Carnforth that they had been thrown back against the engine tenders with a crash. Mercifully the couplings had held.

I remember when we did get back into the Furness Sidings at F. & M. Junction at Carnforth that it was 3.00pm. The siding inspector brought the carriage and wagon inspector to look at my brake-blocks and the van. I also ventured to look and saw the blocks were melted and worn away. And so it was that I boarded the H.P. (Home Passenger) from Carnforth at 4.50pm and had a great big report to make out . . . and I had even forgotten to light the stove. All in all, we had made ourselves a right nuisance that day.

All my railway career during mishaps, signal failures, etc., the cry from our inspectors or the control was, "It took you a long time, didn't it?" And in most cases it seemed to do, although everybody did the best they could to get the job squared up. But we had to stick strictly to the rules at all times with protection coming first.

I liked the trips to Carlisle best, winter or summer, and had some lovely trips both with passenger or goods trains. The little road-side or local shunting trips I hated, and thankfully did not get them often. They were mostly worked by Skipton and Hellifield old-hand guards.

I remember working the Hawes Shunt a few times. We were able to work all the sidings to Hawes, and then the passenger from Skipton would arrive at about 3.30pm. We would take over the passenger train we knew as 'Boniface' and work it back to Skipton, then finish. The guard who brought the train to Hawes worked back the Shunt, arriving at Skipton again at eight or nine o'clock.

This is how it could be at Settle for example, coming back after dark.

There would be some to pick up. Coal merchants had to have their loaded wagons set for morning. Cattle wagons had been put off in a hurry earlier, and had to be positioned in the cattle dock for early loading for Skipton Auction Mart, or other places. A certain wagon had to be set under the crane, yet another wagon had to be left opposite the shed door, etc., etc. No wonder I didn't like the shunts, day or night.

One Saturday afternoon I was told to relieve the guard on a train standing in the down platform at Hellifield. This was the 11.00am Hunslet – Carlisle on which the booked Leeds guard had thrown a note out at Skipton saying he was feeling ill and wished to be relieved at Hellifield. And I was chosen to take over from him.

The engine was also re-manned at Hellifield with a set of Carlisle men who had spent more than an hour in the Refreshment Room there. They were a bit disgruntled, for they had hoped to have gone home on the cushions of the 5.05pm passenger to Carlisle. As it was Saturday, they had also wanted to go out for the evening . . . As a result, they decided to make a point.

I have seen Carlisle loco men before and since who were making a point, and heaven help the man dangling at the end of their train in the little caboose . . .

After having a final word with them I saw the signals come off for us, so I hurriedly joined my brake-van. I knew they now wanted to get to Blea Moor before being shunted for the express to pass, then hang on its tail all the way to Carlisle. The trouble was we had 28 wagons of coal.

I gave the driver the 'right-away'. He answered with a 'pop'. Then – Crash! – we were away and I was knocked flying onto the brake hand wheel. My traps had been placed on the locker and they fell all around, the glass in the handlamp was smashed, and the stove had moved so much that the pipe came through the roof into the van. By the time I had collected my gear we were passing Long Preston, and I knew by then why the Leeds guard did not want to go any further. There was so much sideplay on the axle and bearings, which made the brake van oscillate so much, that it was impossible to sit down and I had to hang onto the brake-wheel to keep myself from falling.

The van ought to have been failed after its last trip. And there was I with the wind up already, just passing Long Preston and knowing I had to hang on like this all the way to Carlisle behind a driver and fireman whom I knew had taken a few for the road and were in a real hurry into the bargain.

We were going near sixty miles an hour past Settle Junction, getting a run at the Drag. And I was terrified! What would it be like going down Mallerstang, through Crosby Garrett, and would I stay on the rails round that little twist of a railway bridge at Helm Cottage just before Ormside? And me with no trousers to change into! Could need a few pairs before we got to the end of this trip!

As we were getting near to Stainforth the old van was steadying up a little, getting into the stiffer gradients. But up front the men were hammering the engine all they knew how. It was getting dark, and I could see the abundant smoke and sparks coming out of the chimney and the glow of the open firebox door showing at the underside of the smoke-cloud.

Before reaching Horton-in-Ribblesdale I noticed occasional flickers of light beginning to show at about wheel level at various points along the train. I had noticed before leaving that we had several of the old-type fat-lubricated axle-boxes which were the very devil for running hot, and the speed we were travelling would aggravate these even more. The oil boxes could get on fire easily enough without my being plagued by these. I was beginning to smell them, also. It was too late to put them off at Horton; we would have to do this at Blea Moor. The signalmen, noticing them, would make sure we would be ditched at the Moor. I hadn't sat down yet, I hadn't got the stove fixed, and the fire had gone out.

Passing Selside box, the signalman was out on his verandah, holding his hand to his nose and pointing in the direction of these wagons. This was a signalman's way of informing a guard that he had a wagon on his train with a hot axle box, and he would be sending the Stop and Examine Signal to the next box in advance which, in this case, was Ribblehead.

If a guard had a hot box on the side of a train which the signalman couldn't see, the guard – if he wished to point it out to the signalman – would stand on the verandah of his brake-van to show himself to the signalman and at the same time hold his hand to his nose and point to the other side of the train. The signalman would understand, and at the next box the signals would be in the 'ON' position, at which point the wagon would be detached.

The signalman must have thought we were safe to make Blea Moor, for we ran straight into the loop. On looking around, I found we had four bad ones. That meant hooking off behind the rear-most hot one, drawing up, putting it off in the refuge siding, joining a few back onto the train, then forward again to put another hot one off. We had to repeat this process four times, then couple back onto the train. Why the offending wagons were not all together I do not know, but things like that never happen. And all this time my loco men were purging to be away. The passenger train had been gone some time, and would be at Appleby by then. Nothing else had gone, there never was much even then on a late Saturday afternoon.

It was a long time after darkness when we left and I was sick at heart. I had felt at most of the axle boxes, the fat ones especially, and some were very hot to the touch . . . just biding their time!

We got backed up and I gave them the green light. Crash again, and we were into Blea Moor Tunnel and out of the other side faster than I had ever been before – or so it seemed. And I had passed through at very high speeds before, on the Scotch trains.

My fear was arranging my thoughts. About six miles at this speed and I should have at least six more hot axle boxes.

We went across the top, past Dent, Risehill Tunnel, then through Hawes Junction going like an express. I daren't apply my hand-brake; it would have pulled us in two. The rocketting old van was itself a nightmare, without those blasted old-fashioned wagons in front.

I could see several little twinkling lights up both sides of my train before we had got to the Junction. I was sure the signalman there would see them and have us stopped at Aisgill. But the back board distant was off and we went past Aisgill like the clappers of hell. The signalmen were all sitting under the phones collating; hadn't time to look out at us. Somebody was evidently reading the day's football results!

I was convinced this was going to be Dick's last ride. I vowed that if I reached Carlisle alive I would ask for a transfer to something not quite so hectic.

The signalman at Mallerstang – Charlie Metcalfe, I recognised – failed to notice anything either.

But my driver must have seen those little axle end fires after we passed Mallerstang, for I felt him shut off steam and put on his brakes to steady us up. So I did the same and we rolled steadily to a stop opposite the signal-box at Kirkby Stephen. What a relief! If my end was going to come I would have estimated it to happen about here. I could tell my loco men were not too happy with me; they were very sullen.

We put three off at Kirkby; each wagon meant two trips across the main line. A shunter was on late duty as a porter at Appleby, and he helped me put more off there. We also put a batch off at Lazenby.

I had been hoping, with getting so near to Carlisle, that we might be left alone to make it – hot boxes or not. But it seemed that the signalmen down there were more conscientious than the lads across the top. Each time we made a shunt the driver crashed the wagons about, rough shunting and slamming the engine brakes full on. It was a very dark night and we were lucky not to have a derailment on our hands as well.

We ran into the goods loop at Durran Hill, Carlisle, at 9.45pm, with just fifteen wagons left on the train. I grabbed my traps, jumped out and was making my way to the station to arrange a lift home when the sidings foreman called me back to speak to Control. They said, "You've had a bad trip, but make your way to the barracks at Upperby Loco. We have booked a bed for you. Book off when you get there, then book on at 7.30am in the morning (Sunday) to work Carlisle/Leeds semi-fitted." I was in a right dismay; apparently this was the Leeds guard's back working. I argued that I was a single trip man, put on at Hellifield in an emergency. But I had to do as I was told – we had to in those days.

I got some fish and chips in the barracks, then went to my room. This was a little cubicle perhaps six foot by seven, containing a single bed. It opened out into a large canteen, and had plywood partitions! The charge for a night's lodgings was small and we got it refunded with the next week's wage. I did not sleep a wink; I could hear men from Crewe, Leicester, London, Birmingham, Scotland – locomen and guards from all over the country; some snoring, some just getting up for their return working; some coming in worse for drink, quite a lot sitting and talking the night away, brewing up and smoking. Apart from this, I could hear engines going into the shed. Upperby was in a big way in those days – king of the northern sheds! Some seemed to be whistling the night away; shunt engines all over the huge sidings complex at Carlisle acknowledging signals. Popping here, popping there!

Just outside was the huge coaling plant crashing and banging all night. Lifting a ten ton wagon of coal to a great height, turning it over and emptying it into a huge hopper, then doling it out in smaller loads into engine tenders. They would deal with more than a hundred tons on one man's shift.

I was down at Durran Hill South Siding by 7.00am. My train was standing in No. 1 Siding ready marshalled, for it already had loco and guard in place and was about to leave without waiting for departure time. Leeds Control had sent a full set of men down on one of the night express trains to pick up the Leeds working. So I was out of a job – but not for long!

I had seen an engine backing onto a train of vans in No. 2 road. The sidings foreman was watching for me coming on at 7.30am, and he told me I had to take this train of empty vans to Manchester Ship Canal sidings. Some Hellifield men had come on the express to work this train, knowing they had a spare guard at Carlisle. Both engines were getting back workings to their home shed.

Following the Leeds men out (they had a faster booking than us) was a pleasant experience after the trip of the previous night. We had forty wagons in all, sixteen with continuous brakes, running as a Maltese Cross train with Driver Jack Cook at the helm.

There was no hurry! The loco men said, "We have all day to do it in. No need to use the brake wheel with a train like that." So I slept all the way to Hellifield! I did not have to work the vans to Manchester either, as a new set of men all round had been provided.

I then had to make out a detailed report of the Saturday afternoon trip, listing wagon numbers, loadings, and destination of each, including the time lost. Each signalman involved with the detaching of my hot boxes would have to send in a written report also.

Another occasion when I was almost stricken with fear was a second trip to Carlisle during the same winter. Due on duty at Hellifield at 6.45pm, I was spare for any job that might crop up. Again it was a Saturday.

It was just becoming a habit, about that time, for some loco men and guards to play sick on Saturday afternoons or nights, so they could have a night off. This was especially so when they had incurred enough overtime earlier in the week and had made enough money without working the Saturday trip.

Coming onto the platform at about 6.30pm I was met by station foreman Alex Kirkbride, who said: "A nice little job for you, Dick! Work this Birmingham to Carlisle, fully fitted. Home passenger on the Scotch in the morning! You should be in bed by 4 o'clock."

He indicated a train standing in the down platform – a double-headed job, both engines blowing their heads off.

Alex said, "Will you join it now, and I will book you on at 6.30pm? Double-headed with Carlisle men on. No need to go down to them. I have had a word with them and they are watching for your light."

I got my traps, jumped on, gave a green light, got a quick answering 'pop' and we were away. With the continuous brake the length of the train

The up (Ribblehead) end of Bleamoor Tunnel, with the date 1874 above the entrance arch. I found working in here as a young ganger an experience to be remembered, although I was not one of the regular tunnel gang. It was smoke-filled, black as pitch and dangerously busy with passing trains in pre-war days.

I had no need to hang on to the wheel. Also there were no fat boxes on this class of train.

It was very dark, wet, and windy that night but, with the stove beginning to glow red as we were passing Long Preston, I snuggled well down into the leather-padded seat to make myself comfortable. The brake-van was a good rider, the best vans being always kept for these long distance fast trains. We were past Settle and Stainforth and into the Drag as if it wasn't there. As we got higher up the line the wind was blowing gale force with heavy driving rain. Out in the open, past Helwith Bridge, I could feel the wind fairly buffeting my van.

A fully fitted freight only carried one tail lamp and no side lamps, and this light was out of sight of the guard so he had to keep going out onto the veranda to check that the lamp was lit – for there were good lamps and bad ones. They have been known to go out with the wind, and there was one heck of a gale blowing that night, especially in the open at the Bridge. It was a serious matter if that one tail lamp went out. The first signalman to miss seeing the tail light would send the emergency signal, train divided, to the next box in advance.

When a train divided, if it was a falling gradient to the rear, as it was on the Drag, he would have to send a signal to the signalman at the rear: Train or vehicles running away in the wrong direction. They would stop all trains on the opposite line, not knowing if some of the train was left far behind.

Don't I know the consequence now! But even then I knew it was a serious thing to be travelling along in the darkness with no red light showing behind. So after passing Helwith Bridge box I ventured a look . . . and it had blown out. We would be passing Horton in one minute, and I hadn't time to light the lamp. I left it there until we passed Horton, but to fox the signalman I crouched on the verandah with my lighted hand-lamp showing red held as near the unlit one as possible. It worked, and it would be too dark for the man to see me crouching there . . . signalmen were never keen to put their heads outside of their windows on nights such as that one.

After passing Horton I brought the lamp inside and examined it, but it was well trimmed so I lit it again and placed it outside.

My next trouble came when we ran out into the open on approaching the viaduct at Ribblehead. The lamp went out again. How I kept myself from being blown off the veranda and going over the viaduct I shall never know.

I passed Blea Moor with the hand lamp out again, then I hunted the two side lamps out of the locker as replacements. Both were dry of oil. Usually I carried a pint bottle of oil with my traps, but was without on this occasion. I hadn't the sense to change the vessel into a more air-tight lamp. I lit up again on going through the tunnel and must have hit a bit of bad road in there for just as I settled the lamp down onto the bracket and let go, I realised I had missed the slot and lost the lamp.

So, from then on, I was up and down and in and out, like a yo-yo, all the way to Carlisle.

I really had to peer out every mile of the way, it was so very dark. And did those two engines on the front take me for a ride that night. In and out of tunnels, over viaducts, under bridges. I would think my loco men shut off at Aisgill and freewheeled almost to Appleby. We were going fast through Kirkby Stephen and every mile of the trip to me was like riding in the ghost train. I reckoned it up some time after, when looking at my journal – we had almost equalled express timings all the way: trust Carlisle men going home for that!

A particular short trip comes to mind. One afternoon I relieved a Hellifield guard from a train standing in the up platform, which was loaded with 28 loaded tube wagons from Scotland bound for Lostock Hall Sidings. Driver Jack Cook, of Hellifield, was new on duty.

The train was examined, the engine watered. Jack said, "I have to stop at Low Level sidings to pick up a fireman off the Low Level Shunt Engine, then 'right-away'!"

He was very uneasy for we had an engine up front that he had no experience of and he was a bit scared of it also. It was one of those engines he had not worked on before – perhaps one of the big clumsy Lankey 0-8-0s or possibly something that had wandered off the North Western.

Two-thirds of the train had passed over the junction at Hellifield South, going on to the Lankey, just straddling the down main line, moving very slowly, when suddenly there was a deafening crash of buffers. I hadn't time to wonder what we had hit for I was knocked down and went the length of the brake-van. Then suddenly there was a violent lurch forward and the whole train plus van seemed to leave the rails and leap into the air. I was down again!

I gathered myself up, badly knocked about. I was sensible enough to know there had not been a train smash. In another half minute we were stopped at Low Level.

I was just clear of the main line at my end. The signalman from Hellifield South, Frank Hulatt, came running to me saying, "What happened? Are you all right?" My driver, a grand chap, came running back from the engine to see if I was all right, which I wasn't. My mouth was bleeding from burst lips, some of my front teeth were knocked loose also. I had a badly bruised head, back and buttock and was knocked a bit daft. Poor

Jack was nearly in tears. As usual – hand lamp broken, stove fallen over, pipe slid down into the brake . . . perhaps that had hit me too.

This is what Jack said had happened, though I may be wrong in my explanation, for I knew nothing about this class of engine. The train was loose coupled and Jack was trying to get the hang of his charge. The vacuum brake-lever was high up on the boiler face and held up with a catch. This had come undone, the brake-lever had dropped down and slammed the brakes on and this accounted for the sudden stop which threw me down. The driver's reaction was to jump for the brake-lever and restore it quickly to its normal position; the steam still being on made the engine leap forward again to give us both the second and much worse shock.

With the shorter 12-ton wagons a guard could hear a 'buffer up' coming and could brace himself, but with the longer wagons such as tubes and bogie bolsters the bump arrived so much quicker and heavier. The larger the wagons the heavier was the 'buffer up'.

Jack Cook was a bit bruised about the face and body, but he took the train to Lostock Hall. I was considered to be too much knocked about and was taken home by car, although I was back at work the following day.

The two front teeth that were knocked loose never did get right again, and eventually I had them taken out. Later on I had a small plate made for the roof of my mouth with two false front teeth fitted to fill the gap. These were nearly the death of me several times, for they would come undone whilst I was eating, or they would fly out when I coughed. If I laughed they would edge forward about half an inch until I learned to hold them in with my other teeth, which meant I had to cut my laughter to a closed lips smile.

As I travelled to and from over the Settle & Carlisle I never forgot my old mates in the Rough Gangs or the many platelayers spread over the line. I was so proud to be a guard and I used to show myself off each time I passed them. I did not want anybody to miss seeing me. I think that was the reason I was sometimes called the 'Verandah Guard'. I used to wave condescendingly to them; they would reply by putting up two fingers at me.

One day, between Appleby and Long Marton, I was swaying on the verandah knowing my old gang were working with some of our rivals, Appleby Relay Gang, which was chiefly composed of Carlisle men. They were finishing off some re-laying. I did my usual wave and they responded in various ways. I laughed – and away went my two front teeth, right amongst them into the new ballast – and myself travelling at forty miles per hour!

I came back that night as a passenger on the up Carlisle slow. Our lads got on at Appleby. Joe Gamsby and most of the lads got in with me. The nudging and giggling that went on in that compartment, from grown men, I thought was awful. Nobody mentioned my lost teeth. Old Wem ought to have known better, for he said, "Have you been having some teeth out, Dick?"

Old Rommer Tom from Bartursett said, "Yes, I thought he looked different." But I could stick it! I had a very rough time every time we worked with Appleby Gang; they had no mercy on a young recruit and never let up. As they were getting out of the train at Hawes Junction, Joe handed me my teeth saying, "Don't spit your teeth out at us next time you pass us by!"

Not long after, I was the relief guard for a Hellifield ballast train working in Mallerstang on a big re-laying job. Appleby Gang were there. Did they give me a time! "Throw your b ----- teeth at us would ya," and so on . . .

It became a recognised thing all through those lengths from Dent, down to around Appleby, that if I happened to be visible as we were passing them, some of the men would hurriedly take out their false teeth and hold them up as a mock offering . . . As a postscript, eventually I had a complete upper set of teeth made, and that put an end to the matter.

Coming 'H.P.' from the many points of the compass that we worked to, was a lovely ending to the day or night turn of duty. I believe I have mentioned earlier the Wednesday evening cattle train – Heysham, via Hellifield, to Manchester with intermediate stops in between. It was booked to run weekly and was a spare guard's job. I believe I held the record for working it – I once did thirteen weeks continuous. I used to get rather more than my share of night runs too, often on H.P., but sometimes I came home L.E. with the footplatemen. I do not remember where we turned the engine, so that we did not come all the way home tender-first in the cold. Maybe it was Agecroft loco, Brindle Heath, or we would go round the triangle at Bolton to get ourselves pointing in the right direction.

I remember, one starry winter's morning, we had got our cattle train disposed of safely and there was a wait of two hours before my passenger train home. Instead, I chose to ride home on the engine. Bill Lewis was the driver and we were all tired and ready for bed. Getting clear of Bolton on the way to Blackburn there is a long straight section of line. Some of the signal boxes here were: Bradshaw Gate, Craddock Lane, Astley Bridge, The Oaks, Bromley Cross, Turton Edgworth, Entwistle, and Walton's Siding. We could see the distant homes and starting green for miles ahead. All off for us, and we were fairly galloping along. We had, I remember, a Midland Compound belonging to Lancaster Green Ayre shed.

Bill was lolling at the driver's side with his head out of the window hole. I was snuggled well into the corner out of the draught at the fireman's side. The fireman, an Ingleton lad called George Howson, was swaying easily with his back to the firebox door.

Green ones for ever . . . but just one point Bill had not noticed. A left-hand green distant off for the loop or slow line; same for home signal and starter.

Then, wham! We were through the points and racing up the loop. We got safely through, but what a shock. The 4–4–0 almost left the rails and we thought it actually had before Bill slammed the regulator shut. George would have been thrown clean off the engine if Bill Lewis hadn't thrust out his arm and grabbed him. I was banged about in my corner and we all had a great fright. It was an easy mistake to make, because I was watching the signals from my side and I hadn't noticed the left-hand lower ones were off.

Apparently, the signalman would have some reason for turning us off the main line and he would certainly get a bit of a shock at seeing us go inside at that speed. The points and crossings could hardly have missed getting damaged, although we heard nothing about it.

With these cattle trains, as with other trains, they were always marshalled with the wagons first behind the engine for first port of call. Behind them were placed the wagons for the second port of call and so on, to the end. By the time we got to our destination there were often only one, two, or three wagons left on the brake-van, which we always left. After Whalley, the shunting staff used to do the hooking off and often had the engine back on the train by the time I wandered down. Just a "How do!" and we were away to the next. Most of the cattle wagons had the continuous brake in operation from the engine. A shunter at Bolton, one morning, hooked off his portion from the front of the train, put them into the sidings, coupled up the engine and then, with my permission, gave the driver the 'Right-away' – at the same time forgetting to couple the vacuum pipe of the first wagon to the engine.

The brakes of the first two wagons left on our train were hard on, with the reservoirs full of air. My driver, in a bit of a hurry, pulled hard away and I didn't notice until we had gone several hundred yards that all wheels on the two first wagons were skidding, whilst the other two wagons behind them were running freely.

We were passing the last signal-box on the outskirts of Bolton and had not too far to go before Windsor Bridge, which was the end of our journey. Often in a case like this, after a short distance, the air would leak out and the wheels would start turning again. But even then there would be a flat place on the tyre and a dreadful bump each time the wheel came round. We went on several miles like this, then my driver or his fireman spotted the sparks and red hot wheel and we stopped at the first available signal box; Clifton Junction, I think. There, we pulled the strings to let the air out. Those wagons were really not fit to travel but we had not then far to go, so we crept along past a large power station, bumpety-bump! Eight wheels with flats worn almost flat to the rim!

I have frequently heard wagons travelling with a bit of a flat, and they can make plenty of din. Still, I never heard anything about this episode – nothing worried the Lankey men! If this had happened on the Midland, I would probably have been suspended several days. I would definitely have qualified for a Form I for I was responsible for the train.

I had by now learned and worked trains over a wide area. I had the Rules and Regulations off by heart. I knew the engine headlamp codes for all different types of trains, the code names for passenger rolling stock and, likewise, the many different code names for the various freight wagons. I was familiar with the speed restrictions, gradients, number of sidings at each port of call and their holding capacity. I also had to know where to attach vehicles on express trains – short wheelbase or long, fully fitted or through pipes – and how many fully fitted wagons could be placed on the front of different types of trains. It was my job to know the tractive power of engines on both express or freight trains.

Wagons with wooden centres in the wheels were not to run over a portion of track near Hellifield, though I never remember seeing any of this type of wagon in my railway service. Even so, this was something, for example, that I had to know. I knew, too, the various Wrong Line Orders, and colours, and when they were to be used. Endless other information I also had to be familiar with, but these points are too numerous to mention here.

Meanwhile, I kept applying for each goods guard position which was advertised but with no results. I was repeatedly told that I would have to go through the grades necessary before I would be appointed.

The fixed rule was that one should proceed next to the position of leading porter, then on to Class 4 shunter, then Class 3, then 2, then 1. After this one could apply to be a guard. Such promotions under normal circumstances could take anything up to ten years. We had very few leading porters' positions in our Promotional District and the men filling these posts were content to stay where they were. The few others were waiting for shunters' positions. The stations that kept these positions were Wennington, two; Bentham, one; Gargrave, two; plus one each at Cononley, Kildwich and Steeton in Silsden.

A leading porter was one step higher than I was when I was acting temporary guard – actually their true title was porter Grade 1.

But there was a way round this leading porter business, and a much quicker way to get to the Class 4 shunter. If I would go to the trouble of learning the enormous amount of Rules and Regulations needed to enable me to take a porter/signalman's position I would get one of the many positions vacant at that time. The line of promotion was open for a porter/signalman to take a Class 4 shunter's position.

I knew the number of lads in front of me waiting to be a shunter would not go to the trouble of training to be a signalman to reach their objective. But I would! Usually, if a man went to be a porter/signalman it pointed to the fact that he wished to follow that grade.

So, in all my spare time, and as I travelled about, I studied and learned the signalman's rules, the Rule Book, all about block working and signalling, single-line working, etc. I had to know all these regulations every bit as well as the old-hand signalmen. In addition, off duty, in the evenings, I spent a lot of time in Long Preston signalbox and I soon picked up the block working and signalling system. Consequently, I was soon qualified to apply for a porter/signalman's position.

There were plenty of vacancies, but very few wished to take them. I remember the two signalmen's inspectors who interviewed me from time to time before I qualified to apply. They were Inspector Wetherhogg and Inspector Wolstencroft, or 'Old Woolley' as he was called. He reminded me of the photographs of Lloyd George. They were so nice and affable to me whilst I was training, that it nearly went to my head at being so well thought of.

I found this all through my railway career and also discovered that once they had got you into a position where they knew they had you, they could very soon change, especially if a man had been acting irresponsibly or made some infringement of the rules. However, in more than thirty years of railway service, I can only say that I found the management very fair and tolerant.

The porter/signalman positions that were being advertised almost weekly and which no one wanted, were not too far from where I now lived at Long Preston, for instance, at Bentham, Melling, Arkholme, Borwick, Hornby, Caton, Halton, Embsay, Bolton Abbey and Addington, as well as on the Skipton to Colne line at Thornton-in-Craven and Earby. A porter/signalman's duties were mostly where there was a signal-box and sidings which did not warrant one full-time signalman or more. Chiefly he was expected to work as a porter, but when a pick-up train wished to attach or detach he had to open up the signal-box. This might be an hour each day, more or less.

Out of this convenient selection of jobs, I finally applied for Bolton Abbey and was appointed, being transferred there as porter/signalman Class 5 on 31 March 1938.

CHAPTER THREE

Bolton Abbey station and Eldroth signal-box

WHEN THE vacancy had been advertised at Bolton Abbey, at the bottom of the form, in small print, were the words 'Knowledge of Telegraph required'. Most stations and signal-boxes had the telegraph instrument or single needle, and in a number of the places they were in hourly use. Now, I had seen the small print but I also knew many vacancies had this stipulation and I knew that none of the men appointed had known the instrument – they had got by without learning how to use it. Also, at about that time, most stations were changing to the much easier method of sending messages over the telephone. I was passed out for the signal-box working but would not be allowed to start until I could send and receive messages over the telegraph . . . and I did not know the first thing about it. Owing to the few trains there, the two regular signalmen were being reduced to porter/signalmen. The elder one – close to retirement – Bill Turnpenny, chose to stay his time out and accept demotion. The other man, Jack Alesbrook, chose to move and accepted a signalman's position at Heysham Harbour. He was anxious to be away. The man whose job he was taking over at Heysham was also anxious to be on his way to a new appointment, and I now had their fate on my shoulders. I was very worried, for so many signalmen had said to me 'Put in for the job, Dick, you won't have to learn the telegraph – they are going out!'

I was sent into the Telegraph Office at Skipton to learn how to use the thing; there I progressed amongst a dozen or so instruments clicking and rattling away. What a fool I did feel; not so very long before I had been working out in the country with the gangsters!

The regular telegrapher was a grand chap; he helped me a lot and gave me a dummy instrument to take home and practice with. After a week or so I was gaining confidence, calling the various signal boxes up the Drag and asking them, letter by letter, what the weather was doing. One signalman, at Dent, was trying to improve his use of the telegraph and we 'talked' together for days over it, gradually progressing, much to the amusement of some of the men who were busy working their own boxes and listening or watching the needle. Experts could read the needle by ear, without watching.

Of course, when we were using the instruments, they were also sounding in every place where they were installed from Skipton to Aisgill. Somewhere up the Drag, we had a bad sportsman who would hold his handle over to 'earth' and stop us talking. My tutor up at Skipton did not like this, so one day he called a circuit over the telephone and had a quiet talk to the lads to ask whoever it was to leave us alone; we had peace after that.

Old Woolley kept popping in to see how I was getting on. At the end of the third week I was haltingly able to send and take a short message. So it was back to Bolton Abbey on the Monday morning to stand on my own two feet and to commence in the signal-box at 7.30am working there until 10.30am, then close and transfer to the outside for portering duties.

Bolton Abbey was a busy little station then – about six stopping trains in each direction daily, four or five wagons of coal emptied each week, numbers of cattle in and out for the several dealers locally. There were also chippings and loads of tar-barrels for the County Council, whilst timber loaders spent months each year handling logs brought out of the Duke of Devonshire's woods.

At Easter, Whitsuntide and August Bank Holidays we had several special trains each day from Leeds, Bradford, or other places. People used to come in their thousands to walk through the Abbey, along the river to the Strid and on as far as Barden Tower. Our sidings would be full of the empty coaches of these excursions waiting to take them back home at the appointed time. It was no pleasure for the trippers if it happened to be a wet day, which happened more than once whilst I was there. There was also some grumbling on a Sunday night when the crowds were rolling back, because at that time no shops, cafes, etc., of any kind were allowed to open on a Sunday.

We had quite a number of visits with the 'Nanny Cart' (otherwise the

Officers' Saloon) that summer. Mystery trips they were for a while until we found out they were making arrangements for the Royal Train, to be stabled overnight during a trip north. Suddenly we had Operating Officials, Signal and Telegraph men, P-Way, Engineers, Loco Chiefs, Security, Bridge Department officials and a host of others fussing about Bolton Abbey – and a big clean-up started.

The sidings were re-laid. The station buildings and signal box were painted afresh; so were all the signal posts and arms. And new ballast was spread through the station.

Excitement grew to fever-pitch as the day drew near, especially with our station master. I would think, now, it would have seemed a big responsibility to him. We had mock rehearsals with engines and coaches, so that when the big day came there would be no slip-up. Even the people in the station cottages which overlooked the Kings Siding were issued with new curtains.

I felt I was going to be highly honoured by working the box for the Royal Train as such a beginner. About an hour before the train was due, however, the Chief Controller from Skipton and his two assistants, plus a relief signalman and the Chief Telegraph Clerk from Leeds, came into the box and I was told that I could have the rest of the day off. I lived in one of the cottages opposite, and I was told to go home and not to come out of the house until the Royal Train left in the morning . . . AND . . . I had not to be seen looking out of the windows at the train.

There were police everywhere – at all vantage points and non-vantage points. When I went home, there was even one sitting in my best chair! I hadn't been asked if he could be there either! He was relieved around 10pm by another one, who stayed until the train left.

Our station master had only one important job to supervise . . . it was the accurate placing of a large bucket resembling a short dustbin in a certain position under a certain coach. A very undignified job for a dignified station master . . . and poor chap, he was never allowed to forget it.

But the train got away on schedule and we were left quiet again within twenty minutes of its departure, with our nice newly-painted station. And I am sure that would be the last time the old place was painted. I never enquired the destination of the train, but would suppose it would be to another new station somewhere . . .

During this time I had been applying for each shunter and guard's job that was advertised, but with no acceptance. Then one day I received my application form back saying that this line of promotion had closed and, as an alternative, I could apply for one of the signalman positions that were then vacant. So I was stumped. Any boats I should have needed to get a guard's job were now burnt. It transpired that too many men had been making the same move as I had planned and the signalman's profession was being robbed of new entrants.

And another thing I found out later. I could have stayed as a temporary guard at Hellifield, gone through the various grades necessary, and been made a regular guard without going to all the trouble of learning to be a signalman and having to move my home. My mate, Dick Bullock, did just that and was a full-time guard in under two years. With the war being at its height, lots of extra guards were needed; it wouldn't have been so in peace-time.

But I took the blow cheerfully and before many years had passed I was happy at being a signalman. I realised I had dropped into the right type of job for my temperament. So now I started looking for the vacancy lists as they came out each week, not wishing to work at Bolton Abbey any longer than possible. My next step would have to be signalman Class 5. The only boxes on my district of the class were Bradford Goods Yard, Selside, Skew Crossing, Clapham, and Eldroth at Giggleswick. The only one amongst this number which I would choose was Eldroth. These were what was called 'jumping-off' boxes. Many of the men in the large boxes at Shipley, Bradford, Leeds and beyond had been in these boxes only for a short time, fortunately for them.

Eventually, when a vacancy did arise at Eldroth, I was sure I would get it through seniority and I was indeed duly allocated to the position, being transferred there as signalman on 9 October 1939. I had been obliged to wait several months for a successor to follow me at Bolton Abbey.

The day before I left there, a box van had been placed in a handy siding to be loaded with my furniture. On the morning of departure, a drayman came from Skipton to convey my few trapsticks to the van. An E. and B. (Engine and Brake) came for it, hooked on, and away it went to Giggleswick. My family and I followed on by passenger train, an empty cottage having been put at my disposal at Giggleswick station. When we arrived there, our furniture was already in the house and a fire burning. All this was done free; such was the generosity of the Railway Company.

The following morning I went to train for Eldroth, where there were six levers: distant and home on the up, and the same on the down, with two white ones in the middle for pumping water.

Dear, lovely little Eldroth signal-box was where I spent the happiest period of my life . . .

It was a two-man signal box. Whilst I was there the hours on or off were juggled about so much that I almost forget now the original ones worked, which made a lot of coming and going. At one period we were 7.30am to 3.30pm, with the second shift from 3.30pm to 11.30pm. Another time they made us work 3.30am to 11.30am, with the second shift from 3.30pm to 11.30pm. Eventually, with more freight traffic building up, we were made a three-man box – open right through but closed on Sundays.

We existed chiefly as a Block Post, situated about half way between Giggleswick and Clapham and could allow two trains to be on the line each way between these places. There were no sidings or cross-over road. It would have been a good thing if we had had these, though, as we would have been helped out of many a difficulty.

The nearest habitation was a quarter of a mile away. I spent a few years there and in the summer months would sit out on the verandah (between trains of course) listening to the birds singing and watching the wild-life all around. Mornings and evenings I would watch the sunrise and sunset, and on Midsummer nights I have sat on the box steps all night – having to rush in, now and again, to attend to my job. The curlews and peewits of those open moorlands seemed never to go to sleep – calling to each other all night long.

Some nights I could hear the trains going up and down the long Drag between Helwith Bridge and Horton-in-Ribblesdale, and again coming over the viaduct at Ribblehead as far as the station there. When I could hear them so clearly, it was a sure sign of fine weather.

There was a singing rail a few hundred yards north of Helwith Bridge box. I could hear it plainly at Eldroth sometimes, when a fast train was going on the up line. I have heard this singing many times when I have been riding over it in a train. That section of line has been re-laid many times, but the singing or ringing continues. I shared the opinion of others that it was an underground echo, or some fault in the rock structure below, for it is in the centre of an unusual geological district.

I also often sat out to listen to my own trains coming well or sticking on Gigg bank, and to hear others struggling between Bentham and Clapham.

In the Spring, those Class 3F Carnforth 0–6–0s with their empty coal trains would be struggling and belching out sparks, setting the linesides on fire all the way between Carnforth and Skipton . . . and the same would happen on their return journey. What a wonderful sight it was . . . a bit careless in wartime maybe, but a free firework display for us. I think the drivers and firemen enjoyed sending sparks and cinders far and wide – and also to save having to sweep the tubes when they got back to the shed.

It was my love of wild-life and the free open country that made me choose to go to Eldroth signal box. A partridge used to make a nest each year within twenty yards from the box. It used to trust us and I am sure it knew it was safe from vermin, for I was always on the watch to shoot or trap its enemies. Long after I left, that bird or one of its offspring continued to nest in that area. I would stand and talk to it whilst it was sitting, and it never did fly off in a panic.

Behind the signal-box was a large wood, perhaps 200 yards away, called Lawkland Wood. From the box we could see the full length of the sunny side of it for a full half-mile, together with all its wild-life. Apart from foxes, there were pheasants crowing, woodpeckers boring, wood pigeons and scores of other birds. At the end nearest the signal box there was a large rookery, and of course hundreds of rabbits.

Just after New Year, each winter, the vixen foxes would start their spine-chilling mating calls – screaming and wailing for the dog fox. Sometimes, only a hundred yards from the box I have heard it many, many times. I have heard a dog fox answer from as far away as Feizor, and another call from Austwick Moss, then yet another much closer to me at Knot Copy. They had the nights to themselves, with the exception of me sitting on the top step of the box with the lamp turned almost out. The bells ringing inside did not seem to worry any of the wild-life around. I suppose they had grown used to the noise.

Eldroth was a very isolated box, though I never found it lonely. I was a country lad and used to all the night sounds. Most signalmen after about that time were country men. Clapham, Eldroth, Giggleswick, Settle Junction and way up the Drag, the positions were filled with local men. Previously they had been jumping-off places for men as far away as Normanton. I followed the last town man that was there and if he had stayed much longer he would have gone loony. These men didn't mind the summers so much, but it was the winters they hated. According to some of the older hands, the place was haunted . . . well haunted. And in the dead of night I have also felt the hair rising at the back of my neck . . .

All my signalman's life I have had my usual little bosom pal with me in the boxes – a Lakeland terrier. It saddens me to write about so many of my little friends because I have outlived them all. I took them to work with me at all times, as company on the night turns. And in all those years I was never reprimanded by my senior officers for having a dog in the box.

Some time before I went to Eldroth, the lad, Nelson – I think he was a Leeds fellow – was taken out of the box there, owing to sheer loneliness and weird happenings going on around him. He was given a job at Bradford. The other old hands, local men, didn't help the situation either – they told him about the various ghosts and boggarts that lived in the wood behind the box and came across the field to watch him through the windows during darkness. They also told him about the headless man who used to walk past on the line outside looking for the missing part.

Eldroth had glass on three sides – but only six steps. So anyone could be inside in a second, without giving a warning thump on the bottom step of the 16 that were usual. Bigger stations had plenty of company around and constant activity, whilst most little stations had a village quite near. But it was vastly different at Eldroth and in wartime there was not a light to be seen anywhere. One of the final frights that finished poor Nelson off he received just previous to my replacing him.

About thirty yards behind the box were several large oak trees and in the winter sheep used to come and lie under them during the night for shelter. Any countryman will know what is coming now. Occasionally one would cough – and a sheep doing this in the darkness of winter can make many a hardy man jump for it really is a deep hoarse cough.

Nelson heard this sound behind the box at Eldroth about 11.30pm, went out with his torch and shone it on the sheep. But all he could see were a lot of horrible pink and red eyes, with no bodies attached. He shouted out in fear, grabbed his coat and lamp and was away up the line to Giggleswick.

Now, he had accepted a train from Clapham but had fled before he received the Train Entering Section signal. When the train got to Eldroth the signals were on, the box door wide open, the fire and lamp lit, but no signalman to be found. It was not until some hours after that the station-master found him in his lodgings at Giggleswick. How the block was cleared and the box closed I have no idea. It was all explained to him and he came to work again.

Some of the old hands would try and scare me, for I often walked the line to Giggleswick in the darkness. They told of a ghost that used to walk through the dismal rock cutting. He would walk on the other line, step for step, not saying anything, but occasionally rattling a little chain. He was always walking with his back to the trains – a dangerous thing to do, even for a ghost. He was never seen to walk on the down line, so how he got back to his starting point I wouldn't know.

I suppose they pulled Nelson's leg about this. But the story does have an origin . . . Apparently, a long time ago, a man had been killed on the level-crossing on the curve in Eldroth village. His head had been severed and was never found. It may have been caught up in the engine motion or been carried along, to fall out and roll down one of the steep banks thereabouts, amongst the long grass. He used, occasionally, to turn out and go searching for it. . . .

I remember a Leeds driver telling me one day about a fitter at Holbeck shed working under an engine and he found a man's hand on a ledge, hidden behind a spring . . . Nobody claimed it!

I may have mentioned that I was very seldom at work without my shotgun hidden behind the locker, in order to get the occasional pheasant or rabbit that came within range, and perhaps to boost my courage in that lonely place. In the early hours of another very moonlit night in 1940 (almost as light as day), I was lying on the locker again with the lamp turned low; it could not be seen from the outside.

Opposite the box, the railway bank rose to about twelve feet, with fencing running along the top. At the other side, the field rose in a gentle slope for about fifty yards. I lay there, looking across at this scene, thinking about nothing in particular, when I saw a man run along the fence in a crouching position on the field side. A few yards behind him another man followed, silhouetted against the frost-covered field. I was in a right jam here! They went about ten yards further, then went into a huddle at the bottom of one of the thicker posts. So, the war had come to Eldroth! Now, I would join in. I quietly loaded my gun – one in each barrel. I would doll them both.

I bolted out and shouted, "Stand where you are, or I will shoot you." My dog ran at them barking.

I am running up the bank, keeping them covered when one of the men cried, "Shut up, you daft b----- Fawcett, it's a wonder you were not shot first!"

It was one of my old mates, Bob Porter, and a sergeant out of Settle Home Guard. It turned out, after I had captured them and made them confess, that the evening before someone was supposed to have seen a parachutist land in the fields between Giggleswick and Eldroth, and the Home Guard had turned out in force to search the district. Lots of these scares were out in those days and it didn't help much at Eldroth. Most of the larger boxes were guarded for months on end by these gallant men – but not us out there in the wilds.

Summer and winter nights I had plenty of company in the box. Quite a lot of the farm lads from round about used to come and see me. Some, who did not get enough to eat at their places, used to steal a few eggs. I have had boiled potatoes for them, stewed rabbits, roasted chicken, fried trout and eels which they have brought in, and made tea and coffee by the gallon – all on the signal-box stove. It was strictly against the rules to have these lads in the box, but they were my type and some of them were a long way from home. I never neglected my signalling duties though, through getting too involved. Quite a few of the lads got used to working the apparatus, and would soon have qualified as signalmen. They all managed to fade away into the darkness across the fields to their respective places of work before my relief came at 10.00pm.

About 1.00am one Sunday morning in the winter of 1940 I heard a slight noise outside. I grabbed my big torch and rushed out shining it about. I saw a soldier walking past, on the down line; I brought him into the box. He was hungry and tired and, being on leave from his unit in the south, was making his way home to Tebay – walking all the way. Instead of getting a Lancaster train from Euston he had mistakenly boarded a Leeds train from St. Pancras. Having waited a long time at Leeds, he had eventually come on the boat train to Hellifield, arriving there around 10pm and then had decided to follow the railway home via Clapham and Ingleton, on foot. He explained how he had tiptoed past Long Preston and Settle Junction boxes.

In those days we had booked 'S.O.' (Saturdays Only) a Maltese Cross train; Bamber Bridge to Carlisle, routed via Blackburn, Hellifield, Clapham, Ingelton, Low Gill and Tebay, which was then forwarded on the 'Wessie' and routed via us to relieve congestion. It left Lostock around 9 o'clock, Hellifield 12.10am. I immediately thought of this train as a means of getting the lad home, for it had not yet passed. I made him some tea, gave him my supper, and he was soon lying alongside the stove, fast asleep.

Later I got the Maltese Cross offered and a few minutes afterwards I got it on line from Settle Junction, signalled via Clapham Yard. I woke the lad up, gathered his things together, stopped the engine at the home signal almost opposite us and asked the driver, whom I knew, if he would take a soldier to Tebay on the engine. "Of course I will, Dick," he answered. And away they went. Later I heard that the soldier was called Ted Mason, and the fireman on the engine was his brother-in-law . . .

I must confess that I spent a lot of my time lying on the locker – we all did. But we were always on our feet and ready if there was work to do. What is more, I cannot ever remember a Block Inspector creeping up the steps and catching me flat out. I was too 'wakken' for that. It was a great cop for one of those gentlemen if they managed to get into a box and find the signalman down to it (or, in later years, with a portable radio playing). Of course, one got away with a mild reprimand, and the Inspector was just as happy at putting one over on us.

Also, if a man was 'down to it', and slow in answering the bells, his mate next door would give him a sharp reprimand and soon cure him of it. And to get his own back he would make the slow one wait for an answer.

Some signalmen were permanently slow to answer the bell. One man I worked to at one time was so slow I used regularly to count thirty to forty seconds, which was a long time unless a man was outside. Actually, a signalman, before leaving his box, must pick a suitable time and then tell the signalman at each side of him.

We didn't go to all that trouble. Our old way was to give each side a 'Line Clear' so that if a train appeared on the scene they were in a position to pull their signals off and let it keep coming. This method was also much against the rules.

On the other hand, some men were so sharp on the bell, one would think they were stood with their hand on the tapper in readiness.

The locker was the finest thing put into a Midland Railway signal-box. What a thoughtful old company that was. Each locker – about six foot long, had a separate lock-up compartment for each signalman, and one for stores. Each had a large back-rest to keep the draught off, and a sloped head-rest at the end.

On cold winter nights, when it was snowing or raining, the winds were blowing and tearing about outside, and no lights to be seen anywhere – with an eight-hour shift in front of one – how wonderful it was to pull the locker nearer the stove, to sit and read with just enough light to do that. On other occasions, one would just sit and rest, or 'cat nap'.

Even the winter nights were not such lonely nights, or even so long; at least it never seemed that way to me. We had our mates at each side –

even though we may have been separated by several miles of fields or moorland.

There were trains coming and going all the time; there would be a wave at the footplate men, and this in turn would be rewarded by a pop on the whistle. Most signalmen looked forward to their work, and being made comfortable for the night. Lots of them out in the country districts could be relied upon to come to work early on the 10 o'clock shift, so that their wives could get to bed, and the lads they were relieving could get away to their own homes.

Thinking of Mallerstang, Aisgill, Dent, Blea Moor, Selside, and my own little box, it could be an awful business getting to and from work in some of the blizzards that we used to get. Though at Eldroth we did not get the heavy snows like they did across the top of the Drag, they were bad enough. Leaving home at around four in the morning to walk three to four miles through deep snow with drifts in some places several feet deep was no joke. I hated the thick snow when I had to walk home after the night-turn of duty. Though I might have had an easy night, I was generally pretty weary by 6.00am.

The signalmen on the Settle & Carlisle line had a very unfair advantage over us on the Old Road. They had the famous, almost fool-proof, Rotary Block system of signalling. (One 'Line Clear', one 'Pull Off'). If they put their signals to 'On' they could not pull them off again until the train that had just passed by had run clear of the next signal box ahead, and the signalman there had put his indicator to 'Line Clear' again.

The men at Gigg, Eldroth, Clapham, Skew Crossing, Bentham, and further down the line had the old Midland Free Block – the same type as used on the Drag until after the second of the bad smashes in 1911 and 1913.

Why they had not been installed on the Old Road as well I would not know, for lives were just as precious on our line as on the other one. That there were never any bad smashes on our line is remarkable and speaks well for the reliability of the signalmen there. There was just nothing to protect trains, apart from this reliability. In my signalling experience on this line I had several nasty frights, and in one particular case, when I was at Clapham later, through a bit of quick thinking saved a bad smash between a light engine and an express.

Three trains had passed Settle Junction on the down line; a freight that I shunted – for the Boat Train – and a light engine for Carnforth which I was going to run through before the 'Boaty', followed by the latter train itself. I gave 'T.O.S.' for the freight, then got the Boat Train offered from Eldroth. Phew! Where was the light engine! So, I refused to accept the Boat Train until I had made enquiries about it. Seconds counted at a time like this.

Soon I heard the missing light engine – a Class 4F as I remember – whistling at my back board. It would be better to get him away fast, so I offered him forward and pulled off. He went sailing past. Back went my signals sharp.

Then I accepted the Boat Train promptly as he was already whistling for clearance at my distant signal.

When the whole scare was over the three signalmen involved had time to have an inquest amongst themselves, which I won't go into. This same incident happened, or almost happened, again some weeks later, but this time the affair came to light – the result one man was removed from his post to a more 'suitable' job . . .

This type of incident couldn't have happened with the Rotary Block. I could write hundreds of words explaining the two systems – one fool-proof, the other just plain foolish; and ours was the foolish one . . . I often used to look at the passengers, relaxed and lolling in the passing trains, lulled into a feeling of security, and think that one slip of an irresponsible signalman could end it all for them.

Our biggest troubles when I was at Eldroth was with 'break-looses' on the down line. I had at least four each year I was there. Some were fairly simple.

The down line was a falling gradient past the box, with several dips in the next two miles. If the distant was on when the engine passed by, he would brake to get hold of the train ready for stopping opposite me. Then the wagons would shove on to the buffers with the couplings loose. Perhaps when coming out of the rock cutting, a driver would see the home signal off right away to Clapham. He would try gently to take the slack out of the shackles, and take control of the train again. But it didn't always work out like that and ended up in a snatch, then a coupling would snap. And nothing looks more terrible to a signalman than a train with perhaps twenty-five coal wagons passing . . . then a gap . . . then another twenty-five following on. If the guard was sharp, and sees what has happened, he can generally bring the second portion under control and get it stopped. Often, though, the front half would go gaily on, unaware that some had dropped off.

The main danger was if the guard did not notice, as the second half could overtake the front portion and cause a major collision.

What buffering up and jerking I have seen and heard, especially with some of those double-headed coal trains with sixty or seventy loaded wagons. A lot of the most sensible drivers in circumstances like these would let their trains drift to a stand opposite the box if they were not being pushed further along. Then they would gently start taking up the slack one by one until they were all strung out again. With an experienced guard riding behind, the job would be made easier for him.

Of course, on the up line, it was just as steep. We didn't have any train accidentally divided on that one, though we did occasionally have a freight sticking on top of the bank, and this would have to be pushed over. But mostly these were empty wagon trains going in that direction, apart from the Heysham Harbour and the Moss Tanks.

I remember plainly one break-loose I had at about 9.30pm. A double-headed coal train badly slacked for some reason, almost at the home signal. I watched it passing slowly in the darkness, then it came to an end . . . no brake van or tail lamp. I immediately sent a message, 'Train or vehicles running away on wrong line' to Settle Junction, as Gigg was closed. I watched – but nothing more arrived, and nothing was showing up at Settle Junction. We had a right fix here. So I stopped the other road. I had already sent 'Train divided' signal to Clapham. In due course the two engines and portion of train arrived there, and was disposed of. By then, however, the Boat Train was standing at Settle Junction.

What a grand place Clapham was at a time like this. No stopping the main line for any shunting jobs; straight over the facing points on to the Ingleton down branch line. We informed the Station Master, who was a very competent man, of the situation which had arisen. We arranged with the drivers of the coupled engines to search the up line from Clapham and along as far as my signal box, and then along to Settle Junction. In this we complied with Regulation 15, trying to find the lost portion.

The searchers stopped momentarily at my box, waiting for the signal from me allowing them to pass my starting signal at 'danger', and then away they moved . . . slowly. A few minutes later I heard them stop at the down distant for a second or so, then – after a long blast on the whistle – they were away smartly to Settle Junction. After perhaps five minutes the signalman at the Junction put the engines into the section on the down line to come onto the rear of the train which he told me was found standing quite near my down distant.

But the seriousness of the affair was when the station-master, accom-

An express heading north off Moorcock (otherwise Dandra Mire) viaduct near Garsdale, otherwise Hawes Junction. I started work with the L.M.S. as a mason on this viaduct in 1932. It was near the highest point on the Settle & Carlisle line and very exposed to work on in winter.

panying the engines, found the guard was asleep on the locker in the brake van. His excuse was that he thought his train and engines were standing at Eldroth down home. His duty in this case was immediately to get out and walk back towards Giggleswick, placing one detonator on the line at a quarter of a mile away from the blockage, another at half a mile away, and when he was sure he had gone three-quarters of a mile he would place three detonators on the line and stay there with his red lamp burning until help arrived.

We had many deliberate divisions of trains owing to some of the engines being overloaded or underpowered when reaching Giggleswick bank. And usually it turned out to be a train that had been shunted at Settle Junction for a passenger to pass, often the Yorkshire Post in the early hours causing a problem such as this. Sometimes too it would knock the stuffing out of a train just to have the distant signal against it at the Junction.

The signalman at Giggleswick would say to me, "This fellow passing me is fairly lifting them. If he shuts off now they will push him over the top." Other times he would say, "This one will never make it."

The rails near the top of the bank were scarred and torn with the hammering they got with engines spinning their wheels. I have stood many hours on my box verandah, or sat at the open window on quiet nights, listening to them slipping and sliding two yards forwards and one yard back. It was on nights such as those that I could pick out the 'songs' of those old steam engines.

But we shall never again hear a double-headed coal train hauled by two 'Derby Fours' up Giggleswick bank. These are now part of past history – part of a majestic beauty that once belonged to the railways of old England . . .

Often, when a train had been sticking badly, the engine sanders would get empty of sand and many, many trains have got themselves going again only with the aid of the fireman shovelling fine ballast and chippings on the lines. On such occasions, when they got over the bad patch and had had a bad struggle, they would go sailing past my box and giving the whistle some stick – as though to say to me, "We done it!" They would have the firebox door open, so that in the light of it I could see them better, waving and cheering, and I would be doing the same – or perhaps, for a bit of cod, I would be shaking my fist at them. What a great big happy family we were! . . .

The worst conditions for slipping were when there was a covering of snow, or if it was a misty, damp day. Curiously enough, a sudden sharp shower would give an engine tremendous help in getting a grip and moving away.

Occasionally we would have a train stick near the summit of the bank on the up line. Perhaps it might be a bad steamer, with poor coal and loaded to the hilt, and the driver hadn't got them rolling where it mattered most – past Eldroth box. There would be no slipping here, the engine just dead beat and not another puff left in it. The guard, coming back to protect his train, would arrive by me under his three-quarters of a mile protection distance. He would place his three detonators outside the box on the line opposite me, and I also set up my signals as extra protection. Sooner or later another train would arrive and stop near my box on the same line. On my instructions, the driver unhooked his engine from the rest of his train, and took the guard aboard to show where his disabled train had stopped. He would pass my starter signal showing 'danger', and run over the detonators – all five. After the guard had boarded his own train, the assisting engine then helped to push the train needing assistance over the gradient and, after seeing it safely on its journey, returned to join his own train under the authority of a "Wrong Line" order form signed by me. Then he stood at my signals until I could allow him to go. It was a very simple operation. The driver in front would feel the light touch at the back, there would be an exchange of whistles, then I could hear them both gently take the weight and pull away. As soon as the first engine got over the gradient and had control I would hear the driver whistle his thanks.

Accidental Division, or Intentional Division, was much easier in the daytime when Giggleswick box was open for trains coming to a stand on the bank could be seen by him. Guards coming back to protect their trains were soon back at the box, and in those busy war days each train was usually closely followed by another, so help was soon at hand. But somehow, with me, all these troubles seemed to be on the night turn.

On the up line quite a lot of freights stopped because the engines were short of steam. We could tell what was happening long before they reached the box, by the slow speed and the clouds of black smoke approaching. It was a terrible crime for a driver to stop in any section without authorisation, or in an emergency, but I have seen many stop twenty yards short of my home signal to 'blow-up'; they just couldn't make those last few yards.

Usually the driver would come up to my steps and say, "We will only be five minutes, bobby. Just want to fill the boiler and get a bit more steam in her."

I would be able to hear the fireman using the long poker or the dart to break up the fire and perhaps remove some clinker. Sometimes they were so low in steam that the injectors would not work. Ultimately I would hear them singing, then a blow-off from the safety valves and they were away again. Sometimes five minutes was long enough – but mostly it would take ten or fifteen. On some occasions I have known the men come up front and open the smokebox door to look inside to find the reason for the bad steaming, finding it full of ash, even backing into the tubes, and then the only course of action was to shovel it out. Sometimes the ashpan would be so full the fire would not draw; and that had to be cleaned out too. They would remove several barrow loads between them onto the permanent way. Then next day the platelayer ganger would come along, find the ash deposits, and play pop, threatening to report them; but he never did.

This was war time and engines were being worked (or over-worked) to full capacity. Sometimes one might be losing so much steam through the glands, injectors and packings that it could hardly be seen for steam – wasting almost as much steam as it needed to pull the train. If an engine had all these troubles together on one trip, it was failed at the next available loco shed. It would then be known as 'Demic' until it was repaired and put back into service. Often these old scrappers were the first out, holding a whole lot of trains behind them, waiting to follow. At Clapham, Bentham, Wennington, trains would be held up, each with a good engine and a crew wanting to get on, either going home or changing over at Skipton for their return workings. These were the times we would have found good use for a siding at Eldroth, or even a cross-over road would often have helped us out.

But all this helped to pass the nights, with the querulous cry from the Control every few minutes, "What are you doing at Eldroth? What is holding the job up so long." They were always very impatient, important and impotent in the Control. They had a model of their section of railway in front of them. Every little flag stuck in represented a train. They were like us down there – one stuck at Eldroth, two stuck at Clapham, one at Bentham, and so on. I had them beat – they couldn't move their little flag until I moved my train.

I had two semi-serious affairs at Eldroth concerning trains. Not really serious for me but they were so for the drivers – it showed in their faces. Both these incidents happened in daylight.

I could see a Derby Four on a goods train doing badly as it approached. Smoke and fire were flying out of the footplate. Then there was a great burst of steam and the train came to a sudden stop about a quarter of a mile away. In a minute it was all over, and the driver came hurrying into the box in a panic.

After leaving Clapham, both his injectors had failed and he had been unable to get any water into the boiler. To make matters worse he had a big fire on. He was trying to get to my box for protection and at the same time throwing out the fire; but he could not come another yard without endangering the engine. The water had all but vanished in the bottom of the glass. He stopped and his fireman had tried to remove some bars with the long poker to drop the fire more speedily, but was beaten to it by the lead plug which had dropped first.

If all this was done through carelessness I believe a man was suspended from duty for a short period. But that was nothing; it was loss of face that would worry an engine driver most if he allowed his plug to drop – even if he couldn't help it.

I had another similar incident at about the same place a little later. The driver related the tale to me, as to what had happened. His fireman had been banging about in the firebox with the poker, dart, or raker to break up some big clinkers shortly after leaving Clapham. He must have been very rough inside there because he got his iron fast and the two of them tugged so hard the brick arch fell into the fire. And what a state those two men had landed themselves in. They threw a lot of the fire out, but were hampered by the bricks. Anyway, the engine (a Horwich Crab) did not blow up; so they were very fortunate. However, I thought they were two brave men. As usual, I had to make out a detailed account of the whole affair in my report, which the 'Eagles' doubtless read and studied with the Rule Book in front of them to see if anybody had infringed the rules . . .

I had one distressing affair at Eldroth concerning a double-headed excursion train from Leeds, which was caused through my own carelessness. I learnt a real lesson that day . . .

One Saturday, around midday, the down Morecambe passenger train passed my box at around 12.20pm. I had accepted an excursion from Giggleswick and received the 'Train Entering' signal at the same time. After receiving the T.O.S. from Clapham I offered him the express (Bell signal 4) which he refused. He then gave me the signal 'Blocking back inside Home' (Regulation 24) which I acknowledged. He then placed the 'Block Indicator' for that line to T.O.L. (Train on Line).

At about 12.29pm I heard an engine whistling for the road as it was passing my down distant signal. A few seconds later, coming out of the rock cutting into my view came this double-headed excursion with two 4–4–0 Compounds at its head, both blowing off. They had shut off speed and had their train well under control for stopping at my home signal. And then, to my horror, when they came well into sight of the signal they both set into the train again with full steam and were bearing down on me. I realised they were not going to stop, grabbed the red flag and rushed out onto the verandah and flourished it wildly with one hand, at the same time using the other to signal stop. Fortunately both the engine crews saw me and slammed their brakes on at once. They certainly knew I wasn't waving the flag for fun. There were twelve fully-laden coaches on the train and by the time it got to a stand the last one was almost a hundred yards past me. The guard came hurrying back to see what was the matter. And when I looked at my home signal I got the shock of my life; the lever was back in its frame and the signal was off !

So, the guard and I went to examine the signal. Behind it was a low wall and a stone had vibrated out from this, wedging the bottom arm and holding the signal 'off'.

In fact, I should have watched this signal go to the 'on' position when I put the lever back in the frame after the Morecambe train had gone through. The rule firmly states that signalmen must observe all signals or indication where provided, and see that they show 'on' or 'off', as the case may be. The signal was only fifteen yards away, and I had no excuse.

Just then, Bill Nash at Clapham gave the 'Block Back Removed' signal, and accepted the train. I told the guard to join his train and give the loco men the 'right-away'. I would give him a green flag also, when I had seen him get aboard.

I added that it was my fault and I would take full responsibility for my mistake. "Say nothing about it," he said. "We will be in Morecambe before time. I will square the drivers for we have been stopped at every station by that Morecambe passenger ahead of us."

Later the guard rang me from Morecambe, telling me in a cautious manner in case of anyone listening in, "Everything is right, lad. The loco are saying nowt. See you again!" So I had nothing to worry about; everything was hushed up. This was lucky for me, for with the sudden burst of speed, then the hurried application of the brakes, the people on the train knew something out of place had happened, and there were heads out of every window of the train, looking out as to what was going on.

I had a bad fright but I was feeling better by the following week. Then, on the Wednesday, a light engine stopped at the box and Inspector Wolstencroft stepped down from the footplate and came in to see me. With a stern look on his face he said, "Fawcett, what happened here on Saturday last with the 10.10am Leeds-Morecambe excursion?"

He spent a few seconds examining my Block Book entries for the Saturday. "Nothing in the book!" he exclaimed. "Well, what do you think of this letter which arrived in my office this morning?"

The Assistant Controller from Leeds and some of his staff had reservations on this train and had been interested spectators on all that I had been doing. Later, they asked my Inspector if he would give a report of the affair.

Old Wooley was in a roaring temper at a nig-nog of a signalman of his showing such incompetence at any time, but even more so with a party like that concerned. I had to make a statement on why I hadn't reported the matter, explaining everything minutely. It ended with me having a day off to be reprimanded by the Head Controller at Skipton. I was also issued with a Form I. Now, it was an awful thing for a railwayman to be issued with a Form I – he had to be guilty of something really serious for one of these to be issued, like swearing at his superiors, or endangering the lives of the public. Very few of these forms were handed out, and most reliable men went through fifty years of work without ever seeing one being issued. And most would have died of shock at being given one themselves.

During my career, I think I was issued with maybe three Form I, and one Form II. One of the former I did not think I warranted and took a very dim view when it was handed to me – accompanied by a rather nasty remark by the Inspector who was issuing it. I refused to accept it, and told him what he could do with it. As my turn of duty was just finished, I clomped off in a rage.

These small slips of paper were always handed to an offender when he was leaving duty, of course. Each time, the Officer would arrive in the box a few minutes before relief arrived. He would pass the time of day, then sign the Train Register Book. The relief always signed on first, and I would then sign off duty. Thereupon the Inspector, with a guilty look on his face, would produce the form and hand it to me; and in most cases would make himself scarce in a few seconds. This way the man working the box could not be under any sort of stress that may upset him whilst doing such a responsible job.

Inside a week I was issued with a Form II for refusing to accept the Form I, and for rank insubordination to the Inspector who tried to hand it to me. I knew I had gone too far and that this would be the end. My mates all thought the same, and wished me goodbye. This one I did accept because it was thrust upon me almost by force. I didn't even know there were Form IIs: few of my mates did either.

A week or more afterwards I got a letter from Head Office reminding me I had been issued with this form and enquiring why I had not stated my reasons for refusing the No. 1 or appealed against the No. 2. I had foolishly got my back up. I was used to the idea now; and would accept the sack.

I replied with a short letter saying that as it was their wish to issue me with these frightening reprimands I was not going to appeal, but would leave the matter in their hands.

A few days later I received another letter stating that, owing to my attitude and refusal to appeal, I would be suspended for two days with loss of pay. What a relief! I was not going to get the sack after all. I would take care in the future to keep out of such trouble.

They were grand old bosses we signalmen had in those days. But the threatened two days was a farce. Years before, this was something much dreaded by a low-paid worker and would have taken a man weeks to catch up financially on the two days lost. Not so me, at that time.

I had been working twelve-hour days and nights endlessly, and paying far too much income tax. I really could do with the two days off for I was doing a lot of rabbit catching – they were fetching a better price than usual and so the two days suspension was a windfall. The irony of it was that we were so short of signalmen that everybody was working twelve-hour turns. So why did they sentence me to two days' loss of pay, when they knew quite well they couldn't find a relief to let me off?

Weeks went by and there was no sign of me doing my sentence. Obviously they had relented and were willing to forget the whole thing. But I hadn't forgotten – and I wanted those two days off. Spring was coming; I still had a lot of rabbits to catch. So I went down on record as the first man to be promised with Suspension with L.O.P., who had to ask for it to be granted! Ultimately Special Class Relief from Skipton covered my two days' absence.

Looking back now, I realise how foolish I must have been. I think at the time I imagined I was clever. Still, I must have had my good points or they would not have been so tolerant with me . . .

CHAPTER FOUR

Life in Hellifield and Clapham boxes

IN JUNE 1942 there was a vacancy for a signalman at Hellifield goods-yard. No one was keen to take the job. Wolstencroft had been working on me for a while to apply for the position for he had a new starter that would suit Eldroth in my place. This new lad had not enough experience to take on Hellifield, but I was just the man for that box where there was plenty going on. "You are wasting your time here," he said.

I didn't really want to go to Hellifield. It was only two shillings a week more that I was getting at Eldroth – and no rabbits or pheasants there!

I told him that I would rather stay where I was until there came a vacancy at Clapham. "No chance," he said. "Those three at Clapham are stickers." He continued, "You would work every third Sunday at Hellifield." That meant a colossal five pounds extra in the wage-packet every third week!

The old beggar brought an application form out of his pocket. "Come on, lad," he said, "Fill it in for me!" He was a kindly, lovable old man that day. Form Is were never farther from his thoughts. I was cajoled into completing an application form for a job I did not want.

I then trained the new signalman who eventually took over at Eldroth and I started at Hellifield on 28 September 1942.

I taught a lot of young lads to be signalman – and one woman. Some took as long as three and even four months to train to the box and get a proper working knowledge of the rules and regulations. Others were telling *me* how to work it after two weeks. I had plenty of time, at Eldroth, to spend in intensive training with them. The lady mentioned above took practically no teaching at all and she eventually turned out to be as good as any of the men.

I regretted, to the end of my railway service, ever having left Eldroth. Admitted it wasn't a very big wage, but I had other ways of making money and that place was my 'headquarters'. To a man who loved the countryside and the local wild-life as I did, I could not have chosen a pleasanter place to watch the seasons come and go . . . and it was hard to leave it behind.

I soon fell into the job at Hellifield, which was a very busy place then with all the extra war-time traffic, and all the many trains that came and went over the old L. & Y.

Set at the top of a twenty foot bank, with another twelve steps up into the box, it got the wind from all directions. It had an old Lankey lever frame, with about thirty levers; four of them white spares. The levers were about four feet long and worked in a frame level with the floor. Consequently, the draught used to blow up the bank, up through the big wide-open lever frame, and right up my trouser legs. It was a real 'pneumonia' box. If there ever was a quiet period we would spread overcoats at the bottom of the frame to stop the draughts, but if it was very windy they wouldn't stay down, standing up as though being worn. Then we had to weigh them down with something. My legs go cold now, when I remember those days.

And the locker . . . how I missed the locker I left behind at Eldroth. We had one each, here at Hellifield; only two feet six inches long, fourteen inches wide, and fourteen inches high. There was nowhere in the box they could be placed end to end to get down onto out of the draught. And there was a remarkable thing about those lockers – no matter how they were chained-and-locked or locked-and-chained with the latest in fool-proof snap locks, eventually a mouse or a rat would manage to open them and root around inside.

But to offset the coldness the L. & Y. had provided the biggest round-bellied stove I ever saw – except one in the Mount Zion Methodist Chapel at Hawes Junction for the congregation to warm their hands and bottoms against, and to help get the preacher warmed up. But that stove in the Lankey cabin really could warm the place up when we had it glowing red. It would hold a wheelbarrow full of coal, and it was never short of draught. We always had plenty of fuel on hand with the many shunt and trip engines around.

I have not a lot of comments to make about my stay at that box. We were usually too busy to catch the signalman's complaint of lockeritis. And it was remarkable that whilst I was there I did not catch something worse – I was so cold on many occasions.

I think I rang the signalman at Eldroth or the man at Clapham every day, to ask how things were or to enquire if the old mountain, Ingleborough, still looked the same. Had it snow on the top? Was it covered in mist? I was still missing the Cumberland mountains of my boyhood and that old one was my consolation for being away from them.

We worked to Hellifield South Junction at one end, which was only 400 yards away. There was no long section here for a train to get lost in. Often we had to draw a train down past my home signal to clear the junction at that end. Many a time it would stop the job for me, but the main line up there was more important than my workings.

Newsholme was the next box to us down the Lankey. Signalman Bill Hartley, there, was a mate of mine. With my guard's duties in this area a few years before I was well conversant with the workings of the various trip shunt and cattle dock engines. Another advantage to me was that I was lucky enough to know all the staff at Hellifield – loco men, guards, shunters, the lot. I was back amongst friends and never a wrong word.

We were busy with our own and the extra W.D. traffic, having almost more trains and wagons than we could reasonably get through. There were hundreds of hours of unavoidable delay at Hellifield, in fact all over the system with trains standing on goods lines or sidings giving priority to other more important ones.

Loco men and guards were working unbelievably long hours. A Carlisle train might arrive with the crew already on overtime, then be required to work another one home. Some change-overs used to take place up the Drag, making more work for the signalmen. I heard of many a slip-up with this. Perhaps Control would ring Dent and say, "Jack, will you stop Carlisle-Brindle Heath at your box to change all round with Brindle Heath-Carlisle? You are the most likely box this morning. They should both arrive at you about the same time."

Maybe the up train would arrive at Dent before the down passed Settle. He couldn't keep the up man waiting all that time. So he would arrange it with his mates to swap over at the next suitable box to do this. Someone along the line might not have got their instructions right, or perhaps forgotten them. Then the two trains would pass in the section. Your guess is as good as mine as to how they would get over that one . . .

My box was a great meeting place of men from all districts waiting to relieve their trains and getting impatient, enquiring and pestering Control. Actually they had a cabin for this job and should not have been in the box. But the 'bobby' always knew better than the Control where trains were. The Lankey had a good arrangement of circuiting all trains when leaving Blackburn for us. All signalmen on that line would lift off and get the circuit, to hear Daisyfield Junction call out, "Ancoats-Carlisle: 40 on: leaving Blackburn", or whatever it was.

All trains leaving Hellifield for Blackburn were treated in the same way. Some would need a banking engine up Whalley bank if they had more than a certain number of wagons on. The following might be the description of a train leaving us. After giving the telephone circuit, I would call out, "Carlisle-Ship Canal leaving Hellifield: 60 on: a banker at Whalley: another at Sough Tunnel, then right away – Manchester."

I caused a bad derailment right opposite my box one dark winter evening. The Carlisle-Brindle Heath engine left his train on the main line and went into the cattle dock to attach two wagons to be first off at Whalley; he then was to come out and back into No. 2 road Low Level to attach a few more open wagons.

I had three sets of points to control there: into No. 1 Low Level, No. 2 Low Level and Cattle Dock. The engine, a Black Five, came out of the Dock into No. 2 Dead End and the guard shouted, "He is over. Nob up!"

Then I, silly fool, nobbed up for No. 1 Sidings. The guard, misreading the dummy, called the engine back and then CRASH! The two wagons which were full of cattle were half on their sides, over No. 1 points, and the engine derailed also, with all tender wheels buried in the ballast. However, the crane at Hellifield Loco was always kept in steam and was soon down on the job. Mercifully 10.00pm soon came round and I was on my way home, a bit shocked at causing my first derailment. Strange how it was never mentioned to me again; no report was asked for, so none was sent. But derailments in the sidings there were commonplace – almost one a week, I shouldn't doubt. And the platelayers were master-hands at straightening out the points and crossings, or changing a few broken chairs.

This reminds me of a real pile-up I saw at Rose Grove yard in Burnley at about 9.00pm one winter's night when I was a temporary guard. I was across on the grid at the time, waiting for my train to be made up. Suddenly I heard a terrible clatter across the main line. A Blackburn guard was swinging his hand lamp with a clear light to and fro, calling his train back into No. 1 Siding, and the loco was pushing wagons over the stop

A Derby Four with a goods from Hellifield plodding along the down line past Stainforth Sidings box near Settle. A bad derailment with a fast-running freight on the curve here in later years "took the front out of the box, demolished a platelayers' cabin nearby and strewed wagons over a large area". I worked here as relief several times.

block straight down into the street below! I think no less than ten went over before he realised what was happening.

I believe I have already mentioned the short section from us to Hellifield. No harm in doing it again, it was so lovely – no "Stop and examine train," no "Train divided," no "Hot axles," no "Train an unusual long time in section," and no "Cattle on the Line," or any of the semi-emergency or emergency regulations to trouble me or make me wonder if I was doing the right thing. Emergency regulations were never used between Newsholme and us either. We were extra vigilant there also, for only a few years before I went to Hellifield a brake van had run out of the sidings by my box, sped away down the line towards Newsholme, and crashed into the engine of a train approaching Hellifield – the van as well as the engine going down the embankment and killing both driver and fireman.

I was surprised, after being at Hellifield Goods Yard just over a year or so, to see a vacancy advertised at Clapham for a Class 4 signalman. Everybody thought the signalman there had settled down until retirement; in fact I had even questioned them before I fell for the job at Hellifield. I was very disturbed about this for I knew I was the senior man on the district for Clapham if I had stayed at Eldroth.

Clapham was a continuous box; fifty bob a week, with weekend working on top of that. They were considered wealthy men, those who worked a Class 4 continuous box. Also, it was one of the nicest on our district. I did want that job badly, but I was already a Class 4, and my hopes of getting it were slim. However, I applied for the job, putting in an accompanying note stating I had been waiting for such a vacancy there but had been assured that it was not likely to arise. Therefore, my circumstances compelled me to take Hellifield Goods-yard.

Anyway, it worked – and I got the transfer to Clapham. I was told by Old Wooley there was no other applicant for the job but mine, or I would not have got it. But on the other hand he had a likely young lad, living at Hellifield, who was keen to have my position there.

So my next move was to Clapham and I commenced work there, still as a Class 4, in December 1943. I had at last got away from the grubby old starvation Lankey box, and was I pleased . . .

Clapham signal-box was clean and airy without being cold. The views from it were unsurpassed anywhere in England. To the east I could see the moorlands beyond Settle and Long Preston; to the south I could see as far as Bowland Knotts and Burnmoor. Perhaps I could not see as far to the west as in the latter two directions, but the northerly aspect included my beloved mountain, Ingleborough, which dominated the landscape.

In the box we had a thirty-two lever Midland frame to work all our apparatus. I would gamble it was the sweetest working frame on the whole of the Midland run. Everything operated as though it were soaked in oil-filled velvet bearings. It was maintained continuously in superb condition, whilst the outside apparatus – points, signals, crossings, rodding, etc. – were kept equally as sweet by the signal linemen. Any electrical apparatus was spot on, and there was very seldom a block failure in all the time I was there.

My two mates, at the time I moved to Clapham, were both coming up for retirement. 'Clapham Junction' was the full name of the box, and we had the junction from the Settle Junction – Morecambe line, to Ingleton and Lowgill. There were two cross-over roads and we could shunt across, run round, and just do anything with a long freight and still keep the main line running at the same time.

Several times each year, whilst I was there, there would be some sort of mishap north of Carnforth, or perhaps to the south. This would perhaps be through snow on the Settle & Carlisle line, and we would have the whole of their traffic diverted via Clapham and Ingleton. I was always happy to know we could cope and also, now and again, slip a few of our trains through. Normally, on these occasions, most of our freights were cancelled in order to let their crews conduct the Wessie or Midland men over the strange route.

We had a huge capacity for holding wagons and in those war years our sidings were never really clear of an engine and crew picking up or putting off traffic. On one occasion, whether it was a result of a mishap or maybe a bombing raid I cannot recollect, I had nine trains standing around my box; two of these were double-headed, so I had eleven sets of men on hand at the same time. There were two inside, one taking all of No. 1 and 2 road, one in No. 3 almost fouling both ends, two on the down branch line, one pushed up that line out of sight of me, one in the long road, one on the up branch line, one at the up home, one at the up starting signal, and one at the down starter. All this was some time in the early hours of the morning. This section could be worked quite safely with all this number of trains on hand, though I admit a signalman with a problem like this had to keep his wits about him and not be distracted by the train crews who came into the box.

Thankfully, none of the engines buried behind other trains ran short of water, for we couldn't have liberated them. If that emergency had arisen, they would have had to throw out their fire.

Our box was set in the V of the junction and we had a good view of all the station limits. Up and down, we could see trains approaching from as far off as a mile. It didn't matter much about the branch line; we didn't often pull the distant signal off for them and, besides, we had an outer home signal from that direction and that was almost as good as a distant to the regular drivers.

By right, when the section ahead was clear as far as Eldroth, we ought to have offered the branch passenger forward to them and pulled all off. Then we should have cancelled it out after it had come to a stop in the station. But the old hands had never done this, expecting that the oncoming train was a run-through so there was no object in holding the distant signal against it.

One of the regular drivers from Ingleton, Jack Bird, used to complain – to me at any rate – that it was poor show that they had always to creep down to the outer home signal and to be prepared to stop at it, when he knew for a fact there was nothing between myself and Eldroth box. So why the hell couldn't I pull the distant off, and give him a run in?

The next time he came in to me, on a damp misty day, he wanted to show off a bit. I had the back board off for him. He came under the bridge, past the outer home at about seventy miles per hour, with his whistle blowing. He was passing me, giving the little 2P steam in reverse gear, straight through the station as though he was Hellifield next stop. He was one hundred yards past my starting signal when he got stopped. I saw the station-master and porter were on the platform, dumbfounded – I was too ill with laughter to care.

I called him back by hand signal into the station, where the 4–4–0 hooked off, ran round the train and hooked on again, then came alongside the box to stand on the down branch line to await his connection – a Leeds-Morecambe train.

Jack was a big jovial fellow. He came into the box laughing his head off, and I was still doing the same. Then I spotted the station-master coming hot-footed down the sidings, looking very serious. He marched straight up the steps into the box to the Train Register Book, then turned to me and said, "Why did you not send the 'train or vehicles running away on wrong line to Eldroth' message?" The silly sod! I told him, for the simple reason that the train was offered to Eldroth and the starting signal was off, and if the driver had wanted to keep going it was all right with me!

He replied, "But the train finishes here!"

Oh dear! And there was old Jack winking at me from behind the station-master's back. My superior certainly took some convincing that we were not trying to fool him.

Some time later he came rushing back to the box again with a clever look on his face. It was obvious he had been reading up in the Rule Book, but I knew exactly what was coming.

"Why did you call that train back from beyond your starting signal, when you knew he should have been brought back by 'Wrong Line' Order Form?" he demanded. He was all for reporting me, but must not have done so for I heard nothing more about it.

The next time Jack came in, the station-master gave him a lecture, and when he reported it to me he said, "Leave that distant on in future."

Some weeks later, a Block Inspector told me – casually, for my benefit – that I should know that when the section ahead to Eldroth was clear it was my duty to offer the branch passenger forward and get the distant off to enable the driver to run right into the station without hindrance. From that moment, when possible, I started to apply this method . . . After all, he knew best!

The other driver at Ingleton, Harold Hill (ex-Accrington), often had his water on to stop at our outer home signal. When he came in with the distant off, everybody had to stand clear. I think he overran the platform more times than he stopped in it. Those little engines were so alive that they could read the signals themselves, and wished to show their paces over the main line – or so it seemed to me. However, they did get a change of line occasionally, for they were relieved by one of the sisters whilst they went to Hellifield for a boiler wash-out.

It was in my second year at Clapham that I caused a derailment there – although not a bad one, admittedly.

One dark winter's morning, I had an empty wagon train coming on the up line. It was getting near passenger time and, as usual, the enginemen and guard were looking out for being shunted at Clapham. Often, if there was nothing due in off the Ingleton up branch line, we would shunt a freight onto that for handiness, to let a main line train pass. If we had the Ingleton passenger to come in before the shunted train left, we would put the shunted train into the 'Long Road' – which had a holding capacity for 50 wagons. If the Long Road was occupied with wagons, we would shunt onto the down branch line.

This particular morning I had the branch train due in at 7.15am, to connect with the up Morecambe passenger, so I decided to put the train of empty wagons into the Long Road until after these two had gone. I pointed to the Long Road as the engine passed by. I could see they understood because there was enough light from the open fire hole door. It was no use shouting to them as they wouldn't hear but I went onto the verandah and yelled at the guard – Leslie Hirst from Skipton – 'Long Road'. He waved acknowledgement.

When he had passed over the trailing points off the branch or main line, he gave me a white light to tell me this. So I nobbed up for the Long Road. The driver, up in front, saw the ground signal go to green, so he started setting back. By an unfortunate set of circumstances no wheels were on the point ends, or else I would have felt what was happening. Consequently, five wagons were derailed before the driver twigged the situation and stopped. The junction on the up line was well blocked, but mercifully the other line to Morecambe was clear.

The guard thought I had shouted to the up branch and gave me the signal to pull them over when he was clear of the points. The Long Road points which I had pulled up were thirty yards further on under his train. All this was protected by my signals on the branch. I had an outer home signal. Bentham box was open and I could refuse from that end.

I thought to myself, "The job is now stopped. I am going to get the remainder of that train away." There were about forty wagons still safely attached to the engine so I told the guard to hook off next to the last derailed one, and placed a red lamp on the buffer beam at the back of the wagon. After doing this he could 'clear off' either riding on the wagon, or on the engine.

I remember the latter well, for it was one of my favourite ones – 8F No. 8081, from Skipton.

Single Line Working had to be put into operation over the down line between Gigglewick and Bentham; whilst Hellifield steam crane arrived to straighten the job out for us. Everything was cleared up by noon.

Now, that 2–8–0 at this time worked about four round trips in twenty-four hours between Skipton, Heysham Harbour and Carnforth. But on the trip when I derailed a part of its train, it was returning with coal empties from Lancaster for Yorkshire.

All trains had a signalling code of bell signals which described the class of headlamp code the train was carrying. For example:

3	Pick-up Goods
4	Mineral train
1.4	Through Goods
3.2	Express Freight
1.2.2	Maltese Cross
2.3	Light Engine
1.1.3	Engine with one or more brake vans

Each code was timed, faster or slower accordingly. If a train was passing and the headlamp code did not correspond with the bell signal we had, we sent the bell signal 5.3 to the next box in advance, and when he had answered this we would then give the correct signalling code.

For example, I might get a 3.2 passing Eldroth, then when the train got to me I could see it had 4.1 headlamps on. So I would send a 5.3 to Bentham and change to code 4.1, which it was when it passed me.

I would then ring Eldroth and say, "What the heck? That train was a 4.1." Usually he would retaliate that I needed my eyes testing. Giggleswick or someone else might then chirp in and say that it was a 3.2 when it passed by them.

Next, Bentham would say, "You sent a 5.3 for that train from 3.2 to 4.1, but it was a three-two when it passed here."

It took me some time to tumble to what was happening, but one day my friend Bill Crosbie, the driver, went nonchalantly jogging by with about twenty coal wagons carrying express freight headlamps. He was the cause of this confusion amongst signalmen, but in a friendly way. His trick was to clamber along the side of his moving engine and change the lamps round; then after passing, he would go and change them back, to get me shouted at by my mates. There would be little or no fear of him falling off the engine, for Bill was never in a hurry. I soon tumbled to it that it always happened when he was on duty, and it was my leg he was pulling . . .

We were really handling a lot of traffic at Clapham during those later War days. The sidings were choc-a-bloc full all the time. Should a train on the down line clear a road of traffic, Hellifield would send a trip down and fill us up again within an hour. They had to do this, so that they could clear a space themselves to accept more from Carlisle or the L. & Y. Moreover our trip that shunted the branch line stations from Tebay to Clapham and back would sometimes come in with a string of empty wagons; maybe 50 or more. They didn't ask if we could take them but just took it for granted.

We also had the usual trouble from crews: "Short of steam," Boiler empty," or "Want to clean the fire." Often we had to hold the trains very much longer than anyone expected. Usually such delays were based on Control's orders, and they had good reason for this or they wouldn't have issued such instructions. On such occasions, a driver would come up into the box in a rage, saying, "If we don't get away soon, I shall have to throw the fire out. I am getting short of water." On occasions they had to leave their train with us and rush off smartly, light engine, to Bentham water-column.

I don't know if other signalmen ever had this feeling when they were absolutely bunged up with trains and all the crews listening and watching for the signalman's next move – but there was a certain sense of superiority. This was silly really, for the signalmen at Hellifield North and South Junctions would do more work in one hour than we at Clapham would do in eight, even at our busiest times. And Hellifield itself, I realise, was only a country station compared with some . . .

We sent quite a lot of wagon loads of W.D. traffic to be stored in the old Meal Bank Quarry at Ingleton. They bore special labels with a red band across, marked EXPLOSIVES, and had all kinds of warnings printed on them. This traffic came to Clapham usually from Lancaster.

One summer morning I was told by the Control that the 11.30pm from Lancaster to Skipton would be detaching 16 wagons of Ingleton W.D. traffic. Soon after 12.40am this train came dashing up to my home signal, urgently whistling 'get it off'.

The fireman jumped off and ran back about three or four wagons, dived between two, hooked them off by hand, and shouted to the driver, "Draw up". I had the arrangements already in mind for it to back into my end of No. 3 Road, then run out and away. But to my horror I could see some straw on fire on the floor of one of the wagons. The driver stopped with the burning wagon inside No. 3 points, right opposite the north end of my box. He shouted, "Leave it here, Dick and put us into the Engineers' Siding close to the points ends. We'll put the engine doggle pipe on it and try to put the fire out."

I shouted back, "Not bloody likely. Shove it down to the bottom of No. 3 and do it there. I don't want blowing sky high!"

They did just that, depositing the wagon there, then went into the siding alongside it with the pipe. I could hear them shouting to each other, and in about twenty minutes the fire was out. The guard also worked inside the wagon, helping to put out the blaze, whilst the driver guided the hose and the fireman beat out the flames also.

A few days later an Inspector, or explosives expert, came to me in the box for a verbal statement about the affair. He told me that if the contents of the wagon had exploded, it would have made a hole big enough to bury 'that' . . . and he pointed to Ingleborough.

One regulation that comes into operation quite often where the railway runs through country districts is No. 13 . . . ANIMALS ON THE LINE. Up the Drag, down the Morecambe branch, Hellifield to Skipton, there was hardly a day without a signalman somewhere being pestered with sheep on the line. The little beggars could push through, jump or scramble hedges and fences, over anything to get to the better grass of ours quite easily. But the regulation applied also to horses, cattle, goats, etc., although I only remember one horse getting on the line during the whole of my service. Once in a while cows would get on the line, usually led by a rough one that no fences could hold, and one would occasionally die from misadventure.

If an engineman or other railway employee saw any of these animals on the line he would usually stop and tell the nearest signalman just where they were. The signalman would then tell his partner at the other end of the section. From then on, until all the animals had been cleared from the railway, each train had to be stopped before entering the section, the drivers being told to run at caution and watch out for whichever animals were involved.

Sheep were not infrequently killed by trains, and farmers were entitled to make a claim against the railway company. The price for a good ewe then was £2.10s and it was the liability of the railway company to maintain the lineside fences in stock-proof condition.

I must also mention here those terrible little nuisances which used to pester us signalmen at Clapham, and all over the system for that matter. Regular little rest spoilers these were – gremlins. Some of the boxes I worked were haunted with them . . .

Imagine that it is around midnight and that I am in Clapham signal-box, lying on the locker, and just thinking. No trains are on the section, but suddenly a little tinkling would start on one of the indicator needles on the block to Ingleton, then it would stop with the indicator needle pointing to Ingleton; then cautiously all the needles in the box point in the same direction, hold themselves there for perhaps half a minute, then give themselves a vigorous shake and suddenly settle down to their normal positions.

Watching, trying to catch one of the little beggars tampering with my apparatus, was hopeless. After a few minutes I would see the needles all creeping slowly to point north again and, as though they knew I was watching, they would stop, shrug their shoulders, do a little dance, and come back again to normal. Sometimes this performance would go on for hours, and oft-times it was the bells that started the nonsense.

I may have been resting quietly, when suddenly the Ingleton or another block bell would ring just once; other times the same bell would ring fifteen or twenty times so fast that no signalman could possibly determine their signal. Now, on the night turn, Ingleton signal box was closed. The block would work no further that Barbon, and the next signalman to me was Tommy Wilson at Low Gill. Tommy would ring me on the telephone, and say, "The gremlins are out in force tonight, here, Dick! How are they with you?"

I used to imagine the little beggars sitting on the top of the telegraph poles, playing about and laughing at me through the glass. Bill Nash said they lived in the caves on Ingleborough mountain, and only came down to tease us when they were lonely.

Occasionally from Clapham signal box, during frosty clear weather, we had a good view of the Aurora Borealis shining behind Ingleborough. These were the nights the gremlins liked the best, and were sure to be about. Our box was centred in the V of the branch line and the Leeds to Morecambe line. The former from there ran practically due north to Low Gill, and the Northern Lights had an effect on our apparatus that no linesman could cure. Either electric current in the air or magnetism in the length of rails heading due north seemed to vent itself in a vain effort to interfere with our workings.

In later years I had plenty of experience with similar happenings between Wennington signal-box and Carnforth East Junction; when I mentioned this to the regular signalmen there they would say, "Don't bother. They live in the tunnel. They were living there before you and I worked Wennington box and they will be there after we have gone."

Wennington was a junction also, though none of the lines ran due north. Even so, those shiny rails, stretching away hundreds of miles into the distant north, had some kind of magnetic influence over the signalman's block apparatus, especially at the Drag.

I have certainly seen the Block Indicator Needles act in a most erratic way in Settle Junction box. The apparatus there was electrically locked and I have watched the magnetic power of something invisible fighting with the man-made electrics and actually drawing the needle in a direction contrary to where they were intended to be. I have been there when this invisible force has drawn the Block Indicator to point to the north, and the signalman has had occasion to put the needle pointing south in order to release the mechanism for the signalman at Long Preston to pull off his signals. On a few of these occasions, the magnetic force has been so strong that he was almost unable to make the needle stay in place long enough for Long Preston to pull off.

A lot of gremlins also lived in Blea Moor tunnel. It was always an easy way to get around a difficulty that one couldn't fathom. But we all loved the little creatures . . . though I must admit I never got to meeting one. And I can be sure that any time during the cold clear frosty and often moonlit nights in winter, over the top of the Drag at lonely Aisgill box and all the way to Settle Junction, the gremlins will be dancing on the poles and wires, tantalising the signalmen.

CHAPTER FIVE

Relief Signalman, Up and Down

IN 1952-53 signalmen's weekly hours of duty were reduced from forty-eight to forty-four then to forty hours, for the same rate of pay. In most boxes it was impossible to allow each of the three signalmen to work four hours less per week owing to the continuity of the work, so to get around this difficulty an arrangement was made for each man to have one day off (eight hours) each fortnight. Before they could put this into operation they had to appoint hundreds of relief signalmen over the whole system. They then had to train them all, but during this time the forty-four hour week had come into operation and the signalmen were paid at an overtime rate for the extra four hours on the basis of time-and-a-quarter. It was quite a good arrangement all the way through.

A few weeks after this, I noticed a vacancy advertised, for Bentham, for a Rest Day Relief Signalman, Class 2. He was to act as relief for signalmen at Eldroth, Clapham, Bentham and Wennington. These boxes were worked on a rota system, which included the Relief Signalmen getting one day off in turn.

I did not particularly want to leave Clapham, but I was interested in the prospects of this job. The rate of pay was much higher than mine. Bentham would be my home station, and any boxes worked away from there would guarantee travelling time each way each day, or booked lodgings instead. I would lose my continuous rate of pay for weekend working if I left Clapham, but on the other hand I would be bringing home as much pay from working the rest day without working weekends. It would be nice, I thought, to be free of working night duties and weekend work;

after all, I had been doing this for the past ten years.

So I applied, was appointed, and started at Bentham on 21 January 1953.

It turned out to be a nice little job. I was not long learning the set-up at Bentham and Wennington, the other two I already knew quite well. I didn't have to break myself away from the boxes I loved so much – on the contrary it was like coming back home, especially at Eldroth. I was there for one day of each week and, of course, it was the same at the other boxes. On my spare days I would perhaps relieve a general purpose relief signalman at some of the many porter/signalman's posts that were vacant on the Carnforth and Lancaster branches.

I was soon back to my old habits at Eldroth, and the rest day job was worth taking, just for the relaxation again. The pheasants still strayed across to the railway. The partridge or one of its descendants still nested between the up home signal and the old toilet. But it wasn't quite the same as when I left it. Most, or all of the old platelayers had retired and the length was manned by younger men. I was quite happy at the job for some time, then the hours of duty at Eldroth were cut down drastically. There were not the same number of trains as had used the line some years before.

There was by then a vacancy for a signalman at Eldroth, unfilled. So it was decided to abolish one turn of duty altogether, and to let the two remaining men work their respective forty-four hours each and then for the box to be closed during the in-between period. So . . . I was no longer required at Eldroth.

To compensate me for this, I was allocated to work the rest days of the three signalmen at Carnforth East Junction. I didn't like the thought of this at all. It was a long way to travel, for I was living at Long Preston at that time. It was a matter of some thirty miles each way. But I took it in good part and really enjoyed working there. But, what a distance! Imagine getting out of bed at 4.30am on a winter's morning when there was four to six inches of snow, newly fallen, on the ground. But in the whole of my travelling long distances to work, for the 6.00am shift, winter or summer, I was only late once.

Usually, when working the 2.00pm to 10.00pm turn at Wennington or Carnforth I would make use of my free travelling pass on the noon passenger train from Long Preston, catching a goods train back at night.

I had a good service from both places – from Carnforth, on the early turn, that relieved early, I came on the engine of the 9.20 Carnforth-

Skipton empty wagon train. The Carnforth men on this worked the 1.10am coal train back home. If I missed that train there was always the 10.21pm Carnforth-Stourton empties which was manned by Skipton men, complete with my favourite engine (8081) or maybe another local 8F – I vaguely remember 8005 and 8145. I had many enjoyable trips on the footplate of different engines from Carnforth to Long Preston, winter and summer. The drivers liked to have me on the engines, so that they could see me safely off the train.

Once I did come up against an awkward driver who didn't know me and when asked if he would drop me at Long Preston station would reply, "No, I won't. We are not booked there."

"All right," was my reply, pleasantly, "I will get home, somehow," and I gave him a cheery 'V' sign. Then it was back to the box as quickly as I could and tell my mate there to ring the signalman at Long Preston and ask him to keep his signals against this particular train, as "Dick is riding in the brake." It always worked; I was never left behind.

Normally, engine-men and guards would do anything for a signalman, just to keep in his good books. And in turn, we did the same for them. If a driver did a rotten trick on a signalman we would all be on the look out to get him in a mild way; or if a signalman reported a driver or fireman, he wouldn't have a friend left in the Loco Department. There seemed to be a closer bond between us signalmen and drivers and firemen than with any other grade – we relied on each other.

I remember a Skipton driver at Carnforth refusing to bring me home on one particular occasion. He not only refused, but gave me a mouthful of slaver at the same time. But I passed the wire to Long Preston then got in the brake with the guard. It could have been later the same winter, or maybe the following one, but I was at Clapham on the 2.00 to 10.00pm shift on a wet misty night.

I had a freight out of the sidings and dawdling away towards Bentham. Another train was coming towards me, whistling vigorously for me to pull my distant signal off. I hadn't the road for him and I thought to myself, "This fellow is coming at a fair speed." I smartly pulled up my facing points, so that if he did overshoot then I had him. But I kept my branch signals on so that if he did stop I could reverse the points and pull off when I got the road for him. Sure enough he came whistling through the platform, past the box and onto the branch line, with sparks flying, gear in reverse, and steam on. I knew the gradient there would soon slow him down; I had him safe now.

When he had eventually stopped, I signalled the guard to set back on to the down line. The front of the train was out of my sight and so he called his driver back. When the engine got level with me, a very white-faced and shaken driver came into the box to see what I was going to do about it.

I think perhaps the biggest crime a driver could do was to run over a signal. This man had over-shot three: no, four, as he had passed the branch starter also!

Then I recognised him; it was the Skipton driver who had refused to give me a ride back from Carnforth. I had him all right. "I couldn't hold them," he cried. "They pushed me all the way down the bank. Don't report me, Dick!"

"If I am found out for not reporting a thing like this I will be suspended too," I replied. "And what about that night you wouldn't give me a ride from Carnforth? Yes, I am going to report it."

But I didn't. Poor chap, he was in a state. If the affair had been reported he would have been taken off the footplate until he had an eyesight test, and if his eyes were perfect he would have got a serious reprimand, which also meant a loss of face.

He admitted he had not enough power to keep control of the train, and if I had not run him onto the branch line to enable him to pull up, he would have been into the back of the 'dawdler' in front, helpless to do anything to prevent it, whatever the signals were showing at Bentham or Wennington (as the gradient there was even more severe than that at Eldroth). He had been hammering past the signals and suddenly found that he was out of control.

"Okay, lad," I said, "I am saying nowt."

Nobody was ever any wiser about the affair, and now I had another engine driver thinking I 'appen wasn't a bad sort after all.

In my signalling career, I had quite a few drivers run past one of my signals. Sometimes I pretended I hadn't seen them. I had many a quiet laugh when I looked at their faces, and was amused at their astonishment when they thought I hadn't noticed. Other times I would grin and pretend to shake my fist at them.

Many a time I have saved a driver from running past a signal at the 'on' position by dropping it earlier than I should have done, knowing that he would have his train under control before he reached the next signal. With the Free Block on the Morecambe line we could do this. On the Settle & Carlisle line, or on the Skipton sections, an outer home could not be lowered to save a driver overrunning until he got onto the track circuit, unless of course the signalman had a Line Clear for that particular line.

We signalmen only reported what was really necessary and even then only when we were pressed into doing so by the powers-that-be. But even they tired of a man who reported every little occurrence which did not comply with the Rule Book.

I never really cared for working the Wennington signal-box. It was too low in the cutting for my liking, with only the bank opposite and a few hundred yards on the up and down lines to look at. I liked to work where I could see for miles over the fields and moors, and most of the boxes I worked had wonderful views.

There was also a lot of messing about with trains at Wennington. The engine of some trains had to hook off, draw up, then there would be a section which had to be allowed to leave for Carnforth or Lancaster. All the time there were other trains coming up or going down. It was a busy mixed-up process, but I managed, except twice. On these occasions an engine ran through my facing points. It was no use saying that it was not my fault – no one would have believed me . . .

It was these little unfortunate incidents that made me eventually hate Wennington. Also the fact that the box was situated on the end of the platform and near the station master's office did not give the privacy I was used to. I preferred a box well away from the station, where I had a view of any visitors approaching and had plenty of time to hide my wireless or books or whatever else I didn't want them to see.

I remember one hot day in Settle Junction signal-box, during a quiet time, I had some rubber-soled shoes which had made my feet swollen and uncomfortable. Sitting on the locker with my shoes and stockings off and my trousers rolled up, my feet were resting in a bowl full of cold water. Suddenly, however, I heard someone coming up the steps. It was the Block Inspector, accompanied by a higher official. Some sort of wisecrack was thrown at me . . .

As rest day relief I was given some wonderful jobs. Often I would be working as a General Relief; there were so many vacancies amongst the porter/signalmen's positions, and the General Relief couldn't cover them all.

For many weeks I worked as relief porter/signalman at Hornby and Caton, with occasional days at Halton. Whilst at Caton I would work the signal box at Claughton Manor Brick Sidings, to allow the local shunt to put wagons off into the sidings. At the same time I would be allowing wagons full of bricks out of the factory sidings. It was also my job to open Hornby signal-box for the shunt, when required.

I have worked the railway, on foot, scores of times between Wennington and way past Halton, taking out and trimming signal lamps. I have also done this on the Wennington to Carnforth branch.

Even in those days, the mid-1950s, we had quite a lot of excursions running to and from Morecambe or the Lake District. On an average

Skew Crossing signalbox was always one of my favourites – a quiet little box set in unspoiled countryside near Clapham. This was on the 'Old Road' – as we called it – to Carnforth and Lancaster, branching off the S. & C. at Settle Junction.

Saturday and on Bank Holidays, there would be so many of these trains running between late afternoon and midnight as to warrant the opening of Hornby and Halton boxes, and I was often sent to one of these.

I was never very good at office work, though I had to do a certain amount of it at all these stations I worked. I got myself into some wonderful tangles with the tickets and the cashing-up. Mercifully a travelling station master would usually look in and straighten the job out for me. More than once it was hinted to me that "when So-and-so relieved here, he used to be able to do the month-end returns". But I used to get into a flap if a few passengers came to book tickets to different places, especially if the signalman at Wennington or Caton had rung me saying that the passenger train had already left their section. Occasionally, when cashing up at night, I found I was either shillings surplus, or shillings down. If there was some surplus I would leave a note pointing this out. If there was perhaps a shortage and I couldn't balance, I would make the till right from the money in my own pocket, even to five or ten shillings, or more sometimes. I didn't want anybody to think I was pilfering. Then maybe the next day when there was a capable man in charge he would ring me, wherever I was, and say, "Dick, what is this surplus of ten shillings in the till?" I daren't tell him I had put it there to balance the books . . .

The last train from Morecambe in those days on a Saturday night was the 10.50pm, the stopping train to Hellifield which, I believe, sometimes extended to Skipton. It was always late out of Morecambe station and there was continuous trouble on the train, often with plenty of fighting, plus pulling of the communication cord between stations.

It never ran to time. Hundreds would alight at Lancaster Green Ayre, more would get off at Halton, some forty or so at Caton and Bentham, then less and less as the train neared its destination. I had worked this train myself when I was temporary guard at Hellifield. I had spots of minor trouble at Caton and Hornby when I was relieving those stations, but usually passed them off with a joke.

One man could not possibly examine forty or fifty tickets in the semi-darkness of the station lamps when everybody was jostling to get off the platform. Some would get away without a ticket of any kind, and many times I have found pieces of 'fag' packets amongst my collection of tickets.

I was usually in a hurry to see the last passenger off the station, blow out the lamps (for they were paraffin) and jump on the train to go home – except at Caton, where the signalmen remained on duty until 11.30pm and they could see the platforms clear for me.

I was in charge of Hornby station on the Saturday afternoon of its final closure. I saw the last train out, and sold the last ticket to be stamped there to a man whose hobby it was to collect the last one from each station as it closed. I then blew the lamps out. Hornby was all finished.

I liked working at the stations on the Wennington to Carnforth branch the best. The weather always seemed much warmer and better down on that branch. I might sometimes leave snow behind me in the mornings at Long Preston, yet at Arkholme or Borwick the flowers were coming out in the hedges, the lambs would be happy in the fields and I would have to doff clothes to keep cool. I knew every inch of that line and walked all of it many many times, lamping, or with the gun.

I got into just the same mess with the office accounts there, as I did at Hornby and Caton. But I must have been tolerable, for I was sent there as relief many times. I am not at all trying to boast, but I was so careful in my inexperienced way with the cash that I was constantly on edge where this was concerned. I had heard of so many young staff being sacked in disgrace from such stations as these, through taking a trifling sum of money out of the till and thinking they would not be discovered. I found out at an early date, even when I first went to Clapham signal-box, that there were persons employed by the Railway to travel from place to place trying to trap dishonest porters and even tempting them to be so. I was tried many times I may say, but never tempted.

Everything was going nicely with my little R.D.R. job, when sudden disaster struck in a mild way. My senior officers – always out to save a penny – thought that now I was working Carnforth East Junction signal box instead of Eldroth they would save a little expense if I was stationed at Wennington instead of Bentham. Wennington was more central.

I was still living at Long Preston, so in 1961 I was made redundant at Bentham and reinstated at Wennington station. And from then I was to be under the supervision of the Signalmen's Inspector at Lancaster Castle station . . . so now I had become a 'Wessie' man.

I remember ringing my Senior Inspector at Skipton station and being rather rude to him, asking if they had grown tired of me. He laughed it off, saying, "No, Dick, quite the opposite! We are sorry to lose you!"

I gathered that if I wished to live nearer my work my inspectorate at Lancaster Castle would pull the necessary strings in order to secure for me the tenancy of the station house at Borwick.

I had lots of little things to look forward to there; for one, the climate at Borwick was kind and mild compared with that at Long Preston, and I was given the impression I would feel as though I had moved to a tropical country! So I moved, and began to regret it even before I went to bed the first night.

I had been happy enough relieving the vacancy at times at Borwick, even though it was a long way to travel from Long Preston. But now I was living there, it was a different cup of tea. I quickly began to realise how much I loved the district between Long Preston and Clapham. Even my mates up the Drag and down towards Skipton, many of whom I had not seen but knew so well, were very much missed.

I don't even know the dates I lived in the station house at Borwick. I believe I was there for one winter and one summer. But as usual the Lord was on my side and salvation again was in sight. A vacancy arose at my old home station of Clapham, for a General Purpose Relief Signalman, Class 2. This was to relieve in a full-time capacity for sickness, holidays, vacancies and, of course, with rest days off in turn.

I applied for this position and was appointed, moving back to Clapham in August 1962. The day I was informed I had got this job I straightaway went to look at a house in Long Preston that I knew was to be sold privately. There was no beating about the bush that day. How much? £1750, with an extra £75 for the furniture. Done! I had a peculiar affection for Long Preston, and, in fact, have lived there at three different times.

Now I was often back working relief at Eldroth or Clapham as well as a variety of other boxes where I had not worked before – Gargrave, Bell Busk, Delaney Sidings, Long Preston, Giggleswick, Settle and up the Drag as far as Ribblehead. I don't know just when Ribblehead box was taken out of service but I worked there many times.

I remember the station-master blowing up the weather balloons and liberating them at the end of the up platform with the stop watch in his hand, doing his stint for the Meteorological Office. We also had a spinner, high on the roof of the box, to register the speed of the wind.

I cannot remember whether it was station-master Bill Clark, Bill Sharpe, or even the one before him – Tommy Shepherd – I was watching from the box one summer day letting off his balloon. I had my gun in there with me as usual and just couldn't resist the temptation. The balloon must have been a good hundred yards off, sailing slowly away, when I let fly at it with a clay pigeon cartridge. I was almost as surprised as the station-master when I burst his bubble. "You silly -------!" he said, and laughingly started to get another ready to be sent up. I have often thought since what a silly thing it was to do; if he had taken a dim view of my action and reported me I would have been in real trouble . . .

One box I was sent to quite a lot, after I was made G.P. Relief at Clapham, was Ladies Walk signal box at Lancaster. I worked around the roster for weeks at a time there, so there must have been a vacancy. I loved every minute of it, the work being different from the straight-through traffic I normally got – though we also had through traffic, such as Leeds to Morecambe and Heysham, etc.

Clapham signalbox, shored up after its accident earlier (see page 104), photographed in August 1968. This was the date of the closing of the box and of the retirement of Signalman R. Halliday, seen here in the doorway.

There were numerous trip and shunt engines, plus propelling movements in both directions between us and Lancaster Green Ayre signal box. The River Lune ran close behind the box, its channels dividing the many little islands. I stood on the verandah many hours during quiet times, especially around dawn on summer mornings, watching the bird life and even once seeing an otter after salmon in the channels. I also watched the heavy traffic coming and going over Skerton Bridge, the old A6 road – the motorway not being built then.

Yes, I liked working at Ladies Walk, although it was a long way from my home at Long Preston. On the 2.00pm to 10.00pm shift I would travel down to Lancaster on the noon passenger train; and usually back home riding on a light engine. This was off a parcels train – Leeds to Heysham

– passing me around 9.00 or 9.15pm, a Hellifield engine and Hellifield men. It was booked back to there light engine around 10.00pm from Heysham and was just right for me. The Hellifield men were all good friends of mine and on this trip I fired on all kinds of engines – getting quite good at pitching coal to the back or sides or evenly just under the fire-box door. With one driver, I was allowed to take charge of the engine completely.

We did not need too much fire to get from Lancaster to Hellifield on a Black Five running light. There would probably be enough in the box and water in the boiler to get us home. Also, since it was the engine's last trip for several hours, a big fire would be wasting on coal. Lovey Bamford, the usual driver, did not care how fast or slow I went. The first few trips with him I would be tugging at the regulator, with the engine going faster and faster. Then I would shut off just a little to get down to a reasonable speed and the engine would go slower and slower, if I didn't give a little more steam. Then she would start galloping again. Meantime, old Lovey would be grinning at my driving ability. But I soon got to the stage of being able to keep a steady pace over the whole distance – it was just a matter of having the right touch.

On Saturday nights this engine worked the 10.50pm, which was the last train back. Then I would be on the cushions, or helping the guard with any unruly passengers. The last few time I rode on that train I noticed the number of passengers was dwindling.

Both Ladies Walk and Green Ayre boxes, Green Ayre loco shed, and all that lovely Lune Valley railway, as far as Wennington, have been taken up many years ago. Wennington is no longer a junction – but just an intermediate block post like Eldroth used to be.

Still, I had another beautiful little signal-box now which demanded a lot of my time, one that was almost better than Eldroth or Clapham.

Skew Crossing, it was called, situated about a mile-and-a-half down the line from Clapham, with the next box along the line at Bentham. Skew Crossing was only a block post, with no sidings and no cross-over road. On the down line there was a distant and a home, which acted also as a starting signal; on the up there were the usual signals – distant, home and starting. It had been a very useful box in the busy years. As it was so close to Clapham, trains could be accepted from Skew under Regulation 5, and any shunting or occupying of the main line inside the home signal there could help to keep things moving, except of course when a branch passenger was due to cross the junction. It was called Skew Crossing on account of a level crossing. Beside the crossing gates, two cottages – approached only by a walk-way down the side of the line from Clapham – were built for the signalmen who worked the box and opened the gates – I never saw the latter open, however.

I do not think there was a lovelier place in all England for a signal-box to be sited than this. It lay in a valley created by the River Wenning, almost half a mile of embankment running parallel with the river, with the signal-box situated high up on this. There was a clear view of the river and away across the fields to Burnmoor and beyond, with no roads anywhere to be seen and the nearest farm half a mile away. To a person who loved the country as I do it was heaven – more so even than Eldroth, for everything was much nearer the box.

As a matter of fact, all those Class 4 signalboxes were nice little places to work at. Bell Busk, for instance, was as lovely in its surroundings as the name suggests, and the station was closed to passenger traffic at the time I worked there. Gargrave was always so peaceful and quiet. The next signal-box along the line before Skipton was Delaney's Siding and that was out in the country, like Eldroth and Skew Crossing.

It was natural that my bosses knew they had a country lad on hand who would not grumble if he was sent to relieve there. I never did complain. I spent a lot of time working Delaney's box, which was about a mile and a half from my car park in Gargrave station yard. Nobody could creep up on me there for I could see a mile or more in both directions.

During the winter months my gun always accompanied me, and many a pheasant that strayed onto or near the railway found its way into a railwayman's oven somewhere around Skipton or Gargrave. Towards evening they would wander in from the fields around to jug for the night in the long grass on the railway banks. Walking in the thick grass back as far as Gargrave, I seldom failed to get one or two. As an added attraction to 'tice them on to my preserves I scattered a little wheat or barley at the side of the tracks as I walked to and from work. It is no lie to say that I have scattered corn, at some time or other, all the way from Niffany Crossing near Skipton to beyond Borwick near Carnforth! But the pheasants I shot cost me more in corn and cartridges that I ever got in return, for I gave most of them away . . .

I got a nice little week in, now and again, at Giggleswick box. What cushy jobs those little boxes were, although not overburdened with a lot of cash in the wage-packets of those working there regularly. Moreover, there were no Sundays to work to gain a little extra money either. But there was peace of mind. They were clean places to work in, with a roof overhead, snug and warm in winter, cool in summer.

Many times in bad weather I have had loco men or guards come into a box in a grumbling mood, a bit aggrieved at my sitting so snug. "If I had my way I would have the roofs off all signalboxes and make you work out in the open, like we have to," they would say.

I don't think I had been Relief Signalman Class 2 more than a year when a vacancy arose for a Class 1 Relief Signalman at Long Preston station. This was more money that I was getting and, as I was already living at Long Preston, I made application and was duly appointed to the post. I could now walk from my home to the box in less than ten minutes. I had never had it so handy since I left Bolton Abbey. It was a nice place to work.

Moreover, the station master didn't live locally, having another station under his supervision. An added attraction was that there were two lovely lady porters; both charming, pleasant girls, who made a welcome change from the moaning male porters who used to hang around a box when it was handy to the station.

My appointment to the grade of Class 1 Relief meant work in the busier signal-box at Settle Junction, plus the boxes at Skipton (North Junction, Engine Shed, Station South, South Junction) and also Snaygill, which was around a mile or so to the east of the station. These were all boxes that I had fought shy of until now. In my estimation I was a good signalman at a country station, but could be a complete write-off at working a box where there was a lot of shunting to and fro amongst a block of busy boxes all within a few hundred yards, with a jumble of bell signals being used almost continuously for hours at a time in the busy intervals. Shunt into forward section – shunt withdrawn – propelling through section in wrong direction – cancelling – engine running round train – passenger train in and on line – train out of section – offer him another – on line also – and so it went on . . . Still, I managed without ever having a derailment. I had some good signalmen on each side of me and they looked after me very well. What they may have said about me when I wasn't there didn't matter, because I couldn't hear! But many a time they would ask me, over the phone, "What the hell are you playing at?"

I remember the first time I worked Skipton Station South, situated at the end of the up platform. The day before, my Block Inspector, Willie Marshall, had passed me out reluctantly to work the box without supervision. I had been training with Tiger Wilson – a Hellfield Relief Signal-

A Carnforth to Leeds train passing Bell Busk shortly before the station here was closed in 1959. The signalbox, where I worked many a shift, was a typical ex-Midland one for the area, both in appearance and in size.

man. It put a big responsibility on an Inspector if he passed a man out for a box, then found out the man wasn't capable. I had doubts about myself – and his were plain to see. As Willie was going out of the box he turned round and said, "Try and get it out of your head that you are still at Eldroth!"

I saw red at this. I don't remember what I said to him, but Willie fairly did hop down those steps. Tiger laughed his head off.

The back window of Willie's office looked right out onto the box. I took over next day and, out of the corner of my eye, I could see him watching me all morning and worriedly biting his finger nails . . .

But I have to admit traffic was fairly falling off around those years in the early 1960s. A lot of the coal trains had vanished and there were not as many fast freights either. Take the passenger traffic away from Skipton and there wasn't much left to do, though we still had all the Morecambe to Leeds and Bradford trains.

Settle Junction and Long Preston were still quite busy, for there were a lot of diverted Western Division trains running to and from the Drag, via Hellifield and Blackburn. For the weeks I spent in each of the boxes at Skipton, except Snaygill, I felt anxious that I might make a big blunder and never live it down amongst the other younger signalmen there. But eventually, with experience gained, I felt I was one of them.

It was in my period as Class 1 Relief that I began to see the biggest changes in the railway . . . that man Beeching had his say and his way. Little stations and boxes were closed, all over the area. Skew Crossing and Eldroth went, whilst I never got to work Clapham signal-box again. In the period since I had left that lovely box got a hell of a shock on one occasion. The signalman on duty at the time had instructed a guard to back his train into No. 2 road, which was empty and would take all of it. Somehow, the guard turned his train into No. 1 road, which was half full of wagons. In consequence it was full in no time but the man, still thinking he was going into any empty road, kept calling his engine back – pushing the wagons already there over the stop blocks and into the end of the signal-box, giving it a really bad jolt. Mercifully, the train stopped just then, or the box would have been pushed end over end. That little episode made a lot of work for the signal and locking fitters, for all the rodding was damaged and bent, all the signals and points being out of action for some time. The joiners patched the box up a bit, but it was never the same again. The door didn't fit right and draughts came in all over the place. The levers were bad to pull, the points did not fit properly and were always needing attention. What was once a sweet comfortable box to work was turned into a rough starvation shed . . .

If all signalmen told of the many frights they have had like this from time to time it would make one's hair stand on end, and shock their bosses . . . Freddie Price, some years before at Clapham box, was backing a train of empty wagons into the Long Road from the up main line. This was in the darkness of a winter's morning, and someone before had not reversed the hand points into the coal yard. The guard didn't check . . . he just kept calling his train back – until he heard some awful crashing behind them. After he had managed to get the engine stopped he went to look; and found they had pushed a brake van and some wagons right up the ramp onto the top of the cattle loading bays – everything had been flattened.

Or take Bert Dixon, when he was signalman at Blea Moor, who got a bad shock a few years ago. The up afternoon express – Glasgow to St. Pancras – came thundering out of the tunnel and down towards his box . . . all signals off. The train engine was *Welsh Guardsman* (No. 6117) with a Hellifield pilot engine leading. Some brake gear of this first engine was trailing and fouled the facing points to the up loop. The latter opened under the big train engine, which became derailed and went over on its side, travelling at very near seventy miles an hour. I did not go to look at this disaster, so my details are vague. But Bert, I know, got a shock that would take a lot of forgetting . . .

Likewise, the signalman at Horton-in-Ribblesdale, Billy Sunter, one day. The Relief Signalman, George Horner at the next box (Selside), had a freight standing at his home signal awaiting acceptance from Blea Moor. Billy, at Horton, had all his signals on against another freight which had left Settle Intermediate Block (or I.B.'s). This second freight, the Ribble-Carlisle, was diesel hauled, and passed through Horton-in-Ribblesdale at speed with all signals against it. Billy knew another train was standing unprotected on the same line less that three miles in front and immediately sent the emergency signals necessary to Selside. But what could George do in so little time, for almost at once the lights of the diesel came out of the cutting from Horton. He immediately stopped the up line, but there wasn't much he could do to protect his train on the down line.

The runaway ploughed almost through the whole of the stationary train. Luckily, the guard in the brake saw the wild one coming and he was out and over the fields before the collision, saving his life only by seconds.

And so it went on . . . I know the state of shock those two signalmen would be in unless they were of a tougher nature than I am. None of my many frights were anything like those two incidents; mine were near misses. I was the only one that really knew how near.

One other slightly different shock a signalman friend of mine got at Horton-in-Ribblesdale during the war comes to mind. During night-time, in the war years, every signalman at a lonely box dreaded the sound of the stealthy foot on the bottom step. We will call this one Charlie, so that none of my old mates will recognise him and rag him. Charlie was on night duty and, even though Horton box was close to some cottages, it could get lonely. Some time after his mate left at 10.00pm he got a length of wire and tied it to each handrail, about one foot or so above the bottom step. This way he would hear if anybody tried to creep up on him . . . Next morning after a quiet night, as it was getting near to his time to go home, he went down the steps to empty his ashes and fill his coal bucket, fell over the wire and broke his leg . . .

CHAPTER SIX

Retirement and the Last of Steam

THE COMING of the diesels spelled out the doom of Carnforth, Hellifield and Skipton sheds. It was not possible to convert them into diesel depots, though at one time it was considered that Hellifield might have been retained as a repair depot.

During the first few years, we had many diesel failures. Nobody really understood them and there was nothing some of the old steamers liked better than to go out to drag in a failed diesel. It used to warm my heart to see a Skipton driver bringing one in – smirking, whistling, and waving at having put one over the brutes.

To tell the truth I both hated them, and was scared of them. I have ridden home from Skipton or from boxes up the Drag back to Long Preston on some of those Class 40s on occasions on a fast freight. We signalmen were good at taking liberties, and for a nerve-racking experience I can recommend nothing better than to walk down the narrow passage from the front to the back in the engine-room on one that is going at speed, especially if it is really well warmed up after a long journey. We had several set themselves on fire in those early days. I remember a Class 40 bursting into flames as it passed through Settle on the up line about 8.00pm one evening. The driver had the presence of mind to stop in section near the road bridge, half-a-mile south of Settle, so that the fire brigade could get close enough to use their hoses. Sensible chaps, those drivers, for they knew the right places to stop in emergencies like those.

I remember one summer night at Settle signal-box. It had just turned midnight, with all signals off for the Nottingham-Carlisle fitted freight.

This came to a standstill with the diesel – again a Class 40 – opposite the box. The driver jumped down off the footplate, then dashed up the steps in a real panic.

"For heaven's sake," he said to me, "Put me inside, off the main line, as fast as you can, before this engine goes up in flames. Everything in it is too hot to bear your hand on!"

My down sidings were full of ballast wagons, but in any case I wouldn't have put the train in there. It was too near the main line if we were going to have a fire on our hands. So I ran him up into the platform, then backed the whole train through the cross-over road and down behind the goods shed.

I reported the incident to Carlisle Control, then I went across to see how the driver was getting on. He had already switched the engine off. Quite apart from the smell of burning hot oil, even the hand-rails were hot to touch and the front cab was like an oven; the whole loco was simmering. The driver gathered his traps and came wearily back with me into the box. He also had a word with Control, who told me to stop the Ancoats-Glasgow freight, which was just leaving Hellifield, to pick up the driver who would travel in the brake to Carlisle and lodge for his back working that day. He told me, "I am just turned sixty years, but feel like seventy." And he looked it, I thought. He said he was at an awkward age to take his redundancy, so had decided to take on the diesels. He had only been driving them for a little over a year and was almost a nervous wreck. To make matters worse, most of his driving now was on single-manned engines. All his life he had been used to having a mate on the footplate with him – now he was all alone on a powerful machine he didn't understand. I knew his train was running late, and no wonder, when he told me this was the third loco that had failed with him on this trip since leaving Nottingham.

Truth to tell, the only thing about the diesels I did like to hear was a driver trying to play "On Ilkley Moor ba'at 'at" on the two-toned horn.

I was on night duty at the Engine Shed box, Skipton, the day the shed was officially booked to close. We had a notice in the box stating that no more locomotives in steam had to leave the shed after that date. The authorities went all out to get them removed from their duties, scrapped, and out of sight – just anywhere. However, a few were simply compelled to come back into action on occasion, owing to the failures or scarcity of the diesels. I, myself, had a few in and out again on the few times I worked that box afterwards.

Around midnight I had a favourite Black Five come on to the shed to lie down and die after working its last job somewhere. The driver, a young chap who had been transferred to Skipton from Hellifield when the latter closed, stopped near the signal box window and handed me his lunch bag for a handy pick-up after he had disposed of his engine. A few minutes later he came to collect it. His words to me were, "Well, that is the last of those old iron bastards that I hope to drive." How that remark rankled with me, and still does . . .

No more engines on or off the shed that night, not for me anyway. Nothing to do but sleep . . . but I didn't feel like sleeping. Around one a.m. I thought I would have a quick look round the shed on my own; I knew there was only one man on duty there, and he wouldn't mind.

The place was in darkness, but I soon found some light switches and lit the place up. To me it was indeed a sad place – at the back of the shed were several cold dead engines. Others were scattered here and there, in the process of dying down . . . just simmering quietly, their fires almost burnt out. It seemed like a giant graveyard – just as though these great innocent creatures had been brought here to die against their will.

Immediately outside the shed, in No. 1 Road, was the Black Five I had turned in earlier. I went up on top. Everything was shut, except the cylinder taps. There was just a faint glow of fire in the box, left just as it was when it came in. She was still simmering and sizzling lightly. I looked at the steam gauge; still more than fifty pounds showing – enough to blow the whistle. I couldn't resist it. Around 1.30am on a Sunday morning, everybody in Skipton should be sleeping. I know the other four signalmen on duty around the station would have been trying to sleep. So, I gave a 'Tally Ho' on the old engine whistle. I gave it more than that. I ended up with 'The Runaway Train Came Over the Hill, and She Blew . . .'.

I reckon my mates all jumped off their lockers, thinking they had one on their hands, and looked at their Block Indicators in fear. I didn't worry, for I knew nothing had left Leeds, Aisgill or Morecambe when I had left my box.

It was heard all over Skipton – but nobody ever fathomed the cause. I have wished ever since that I had screwed the whistle off that engine and kept it as a souvenir; no one would have missed it.

Mention of the whistle of a runaway train reminds me we signalmen often heard what we thought was a runaway whistle, or a driver whistling in alarm, and then later found it was caused by steam leaking into a whistle, causing it to sound off intermittently.

I remember the Ingleton branch goods coming into Clapham station with the engine pop-popping one time. I knew there was no alarm, for the signalman at Low Gill had warned me the crew couldn't stop the whistle crowing. They must not have had a shut-off valve. The fireman – a Scot named Tom Rennie – was so incensed with the noise when they stopped near me that he climbed up on top of the boiler and gave the whistle a bang with his coal hammer. This put new life into it, and it knocked the whistle off altogether. This stopped its noise but how they stopped the steam escaping, I do not know.

I will tell, now, of a real runaway train on the Drag. This incident happened sometime during the last War: but for once it happened in daylight. I was not concerned with it in any way but was on duty at the time, hidden safely away at Eldroth on the Old Road.

The train concerned was a Block, loaded with 'Monkey muck' (otherwise iron ore) from the Central Division, via Blackburn and Hellifield, bound for Scotland. Having stopped at Blea Moor, it was shunted through the cross-over onto the up line for the passage of an express.

Safely across the road, the engine must have pulled up with a jerk, for a coupling near the front snapped whereupon the remainder of the train started running back towards Ribblehead station, the brake van leading. The guard applied his hand brake, screwing it down as tight as he could but found it wouldn't hold the twenty or more wagons of heavy iron ore. So . . . sensible fellow that he was . . . he baled out.

Away the train of wagons went, gathering speed all the time and on past Ribblehead, Selside, Horton-in-Ribblesdale, Helwith Bridge, Stainforth Sidings, Settle and Settle Junction boxes, on a steady falling gradient all the way.

Almost every day for months, excepting that day, the Horton shunt had occupied the up main line there until after the express had run through. It is awful to imagine what would have happened if it had been standing there.

I remember the signalman on duty at Stainforth Sidings box telling me he got his emergency signals on in good time, then he left the box and ran well back into the sidings in case the train should become derailed on the sharp curve outside. But he said it passed like an express passenger train, and steady as a rock. The total distance run must have been almost twenty miles, all of it downhill, excepting the last half mile, where there was a piece of rising gradient between Settle Junction and Long Preston and the runaway ran itself to a stop. What a relief to all concerned! It was a miracle that no other train was concerned and no terrible crash took place.

That signalman at Stainforth must have often had doubts about the nearness of his box to the main line and his fears were justified not many years afterwards, for a bad derailment there with a fast-running freight took the front out of the box, demolished a platelayers' cabin nearby and strewed wagons over a large area.

By this date I was losing interest in my job fast. Practically all my favourite signal boxes on the Old Road had gone. The rewards for working long hours were being taken away from me. Everything all around seemed to be falling to pieces, sidings taken out, scrap lying around.

Even a lot of my mates seemed to be of an alien nature. All the older end of all grades – locos, guards, platelayers, signalmen – had retired or died. I could count on my fingers, and still have some spare, how many older men than me were left in the boxes. And I found that temper of mine seemed to flare up sharper and oftener than it ought to . . .

At this period the Railway Executive Estates Department was having a selling campaign for bits of railway property: station houses, former waiting rooms, plots of land, etc. Though I was still living at Long Preston, I was interested in what was going on in and around Clapham, for I had put in a large slice of my life around there. The Ingleton branch had been officially closed and the last emergency diversion had run. About one mile and a half from Clapham station, up that branch line, is a tiny hamlet called Green Close, surrounded by the moorland ground called Newby Moors and Clapham Common: seven hundred and eighty acres of it. The line ran through the middle of it, with a small farm at each side, and on a piece of spare land on the side were three old railway cottages empty and falling into decay. The land they stood in was almost two acres.

For something like two years I had been negotiating to buy the old houses and this land. Keeping my fingers crossed, I managed to close the deal in early 1966. Then I put in for planning permission to pull them down and build a bungalow on the place where they stood. After a long anxious wait, this was granted. So then began a hard and tedious time, for I would build the bungalow out of the stone of the old houses myself, with the help of my wife. Something I have never mentioned during these writings is the gift I have been blessed with in working in stone, going right back to my days on Moorcock Viaduct, though I desire to be modest.

In the September of 1966, with the help of my wife and an old Ellis Chalmers tractor, I pulled and tugged, heaved and swore until the poor old railway houses were razed to the ground. It was sad really, for they had been the homes of some families through many hundreds of years. I remember when they were lived in, and could name the last three tenants.

During the building that followed we had quite a bit of activity on the line outside – our poor old branch was dying at the rate of nearly a mile a day, the contractors removing the rails and sleepers came from Clapham with a long material train, either drawn or pushed by two engines. They first took up the track of the up line and then worked from the Low Gill end to pick up the down line. Each time the empty or the full train was passing, I went to the top of the embankment to give the lads a wave.

On the last day they passed me, I had a few moments talking to the loco men (from Carnforth) and the guard. I said to the driver, "Give me a tattoo on your whistle as you go under the bridge. Whistle 'Good-bye' like." He did, and that was the last train from the branch to run under my bridge. A few days later all evidence of there ever having been a track had gone . . .

After many long hours of work during a wet summer, we moved in at the beginning of April 1968 . . . "Not bad for two pair of hands," says I. Before that, however, I regret to say I had resigned from the railway service . . .